A CAL

HONEST

by Reason and God's Amazing Grace

DOUBTS
RESOLVED

DAVE HUNT

BEND • OREGON

Except where otherwise indicated, all Scripture quotations in this book are taken from the King James Version of the Bible.

Italics used in Scripture references are added for emphasis by the author.

A free monthly newsletter, THE BEREAN CALL, *may be received by sending a request to the address below, or by calling 1-800-937-6638.*

To register for free e-mail updates, to access our digital archives, and to order a variety of additional resource materials online, visit us at: *www.thebereancall.org*

HONEST DOUBTS—RESOLVED
Copyright © 2005 by Dave Hunt
Published by The Berean Call
PO Box 7019, Bend, OR 97708

ISBN: 1-928660-34-7
Library of Congress Control Number: 2005928879

Printed in the United States of America.

CONTENTS

Publisher's Note

The paperback you hold in your hands has been produced in response to thousands of readers of *The Berean Call* (our monthly newsletter) and listeners of *Search the Scriptures Daily* (our weekly radio broadcast) who have requested a short and simple-to-understand introduction to the complicated and confusing teachings of Calvinism.

The twelve chapters in this book are derived from material taken from just three chapters of Dave Hunt's much larger and comprehensive work on Calvinism entitled *What Love Is This? Calvinism's Misrepresentation of God*, which we recommend for a thorough biblical study of the critical theological details. (For more information on this 576-page volume, see the resource section in the back of this book.)

Although the dialogue between Al and Jan in *A Calvinist's Honest Doubts* is fictionalized, the subject matter—and the arguments and answers presented—are entirely real and rational. As such, Al and Jan's dialogue and thought processes are composites of "real life" situations and circumstances, drawn from the comments and experiences of real people who have written to or spoken with the author.

So, whether you are a minister already familiar with the issues or are simply seeking the Truth of God's Word with regard to Calvinism, it is our sincere prayer that you will be blessed by the content and unique format of this book—and that afterward you will truly know God's love and grace in a deeper and more meaningful way. —TBC

chapter

WHY THIS BOOK?

"CAN YOU ANSWER SOME QUESTIONS about Calvinism?" The query came to me from a young man sitting with me and several others at a restaurant in a city where I was speaking at a conference.[1]

"Why do you ask *me?*"

"We heard you were writing a book about Calvinism."

"Yes, I am—a book, in fact, that I didn't want to write. There are fine Christians on both sides. The last thing I want to do is create more controversy—but it's a topic that really has to be faced and dealt with thoroughly." Glancing around the table, I was surprised at the sudden interest reflected on each face. Everyone was listening intently.

"I had scarcely given Calvinism a thought for years. Then suddenly—or so it seemed to me—in the last few years

Calvinism has emerged as an issue everywhere. Perhaps I'm just waking up, but it seems to me that this particular doctrine is being promoted far more widely and aggressively now than I was ever aware of in the past."

A Spreading Influence

"Our church recently added a new associate pastor to the staff—a graduate of the Master's College and Seminary in Southern California," explained the young man. "He introduces Calvinism in almost every session in his Bible class, though most of the people don't seem to recognize it."

"Let me suggest how he might do it," I responded. "He asks the class what they think comes first, faith or regeneration. Everyone says, 'Faith, of course—believe on the Lord Jesus Christ and thou shalt be saved.' Then he challenges them, 'But mankind is dead in trespasses and sins. How can a dead man believe?'"

I had the young man's total attention. "That's it exactly! How did you know?"

"Then he explains," I continued, "that God has to give life sovereignly to those who are spiritually dead before they can believe or even understand the gospel—that *regeneration* must precede faith."

"You're right! But it seems bizarre...like having to get saved before you can get saved!"

"The Calvinist wouldn't put it in those precise words," I responded, "but it's even a bit stranger than that. Without understanding or believing anything about God or Christ or the Bible—because the 'totally depraved' supposedly can't until they're regenerated—the 'elect' are made spiritually alive by sovereign regeneration from God without any desire or cooperation on their part and without even knowing what is happening to them at the time."

"That's exactly what he's been teaching," added another member of the same church. "It doesn't make sense. I never read anything like that in the Bible."

"Are you the only ones who have expressed any concern?" I asked. "Do those who thought that faith came first accept this new concept immediately?"

"Most do. But it *has* caused some confusion. And a few people have left the church."

"No one challenges him," I asked, "with the obvious fact that spiritual death can't be equated with physical death? That *physically* dead people not only can't believe but can't sin or do anything else?"

"I guess none of us have thought of that."

"What does the senior pastor say?"

"He doesn't seem to know how to handle the confusion. We never heard anything like this from the pulpit before, but now hints of Calvinism are even finding their way into *his* sermons."

A Growing Concern

The conversation went on like this for some time. Every new aspect of Calvinism I explained was greeted with further exclamations of "Yes! That's exactly what we're hearing."

Others, from entirely different areas of the country, began to relate their experiences. One man had recently left a church that had split over Calvinism. The deacon board had voted that every member must sign a Calvinistic statement of faith. Someone else came from a church whose pastor and elders had taken a hard line against what they considered a divisive issue and had disfellowshiped a Sunday school teacher for influencing his junior high class with Calvinism, in spite of several warnings not to teach it. Another couple had visited a highly recommended church in a large city near their home, pastored by a well-known Calvinist author.

"We don't really know much about Calvinism," my dinner companions confessed. "But it was a strange experience. On the one hand, we had the impression that these people felt certain they were the *elect*. Yet there also seemed to be some insecurity, as though performance were a major evidence of one's salvation."

As we got up to leave, a young woman who had sat through the entire discussion in silence asked if she could have a private moment of my time. We sat down again, and she began a tale of grief. She was a pastor's wife. Their lives and ministry had been happy and fruitful until her husband and two close friends, also pastors, became interested in a new "truth." All three were aspiring "intellectuals." As a result of reading current Calvinist authors they had been drawn to the writings of John Calvin, Jonathan Edwards, John Knox, and others.

Tragic Results

Their study, taking them all the way back to Augustine, eventually became almost an obsession. Then each of them began to preach this new "light" from their pulpits. After being warned several times to desist, they were removed from their pastorates. Eventually, her husband began to worry whether he was really one of the elect. The nagging questions grew into full-blown doubts about his salvation. Calvinism, which had once seemed so satisfying, now began to haunt him with uncertainty. Was he really one of the elect?

"You were never drawn into it?" I asked.

She shook her head. "I'm not an intellectual—which may be why it never appealed to me. But isn't God supposed to be a God of love? In my simple mind it didn't make sense that the God of the Bible didn't love everyone enough to want them all in heaven, that Christ hadn't died for everyone even though the Bible seemed to say that He had."

Tears came to her eyes. With effort she continued, "I kept trying to tell my husband that the God he now believed in and wanted to preach about—a God who predestined people before they were even born to spend eternity in the Lake of Fire—was not the God I knew and loved."

Troubling encounters such as these became more frequent and soon demanded deeper insight on my part into a system that was obviously embraced by a larger portion of the church than I had realized. It seemed so alien to everything I had believed about a God whose sovereignty did not diminish His mercy and love. My heart went out to such people, whom I was increasingly encountering. I wanted to do something to help them and the many others facing the same conflict whom I would probably never meet.

---

1. Narration represents a composite of several of the author's recent actual experiences.

chapter 2

AN ISSUE OF GREAT IMPORTANCE

CALVINISM HAS NEVER SEEMED BIBLICAL to me for a number of reasons. Over the years, my considerable objections have been discussed privately and in detail with several friends who are staunch Calvinists. Thankfully, in spite of our serious differences and our inability to resolve them, there was never any loss of good will. We remain in close friendship to this day and simply avoid this subject.

It is true that "throughout history many of the great evangelists, missionaries, and stalwart theologians held to the...doctrines of grace known as Calvinism."[1] R. C. Sproul declares that "the titans of classical Christian scholarship" are Calvinists.[2] The additional claim is often made that, although many have not made it known publicly, most of today's leading evangelicals in America hold to some form of this doctrine. I soon discovered that there were far more books in print promoting Calvinism than I had ever imagined. Their number and influence are growing rapidly.

The *New Geneva Study Bible* aggressively promotes Calvinism in its marginal explanations of key passages. It claims to present "Reformation truth." That bold phrase equates the Reformation with Calvinism—a proposition that is almost universally accepted among evangelicals today. The question of whether this is true is surely one of great importance.

A Cause of Greater Concern

The significance of our concern is given further weight by the fact that its proponents even claim that "Calvinism is pure biblical Christianity in its clearest and purest expression."[3] D. James Kennedy has said, "I am a Presbyterian because I believe Presbyterianism is the purest form of Calvinism."[4] John Piper writes, "The doctrines of grace (Total depravity, Unconditional election, Limited atonement, Irresistible grace, Perseverance of the saints) are the warp and woof of the biblical gospel cherished by so many saints for centuries."[5]

Wouldn't this mean, then, that those who do not preach Calvinism do not preach the gospel? And how could evangelicals possibly be saved who reject the five points of Calvinism that Piper claims are "the warp and woof of the biblical gospel"? C. H. Spurgeon, who at times contradicted Calvinism, declared:

> Those great truths, which are called Calvinism...are, I believe, the essential doctrines of the Gospel that is in Jesus Christ. Now I do not ask whether you believe all this [Calvinism]. It is possible you may not. But I believe you will before you enter heaven. I am persuaded that as

> God may have washed your hearts, He will wash your
> brains before you enter heaven.[6]

Such a strong statement is impressive, coming from Charles Haddon Spurgeon. John H. Gerstner writes, "We believe with the great Baptist preacher, Charles Haddon Spurgeon, that Calvinism is just another name for Christianity."[7] Again, if Calvinism is true Christianity, would that mean that those who do not accept its "Five Points" are not Christians? Surely, most Calvinists would not say so, but isn't the implication there? And how many of these points must one accept to be saved?

Good Men on Both Sides

Of course, there were many Christian leaders of equal stature in the history of the church, such as D. L. Moody, who were of the opposite opinion. Norman F. Douty lists more than seventy Christian leaders who, in whole or in part, opposed Calvinism (especially its doctrine of Limited Atonement)—among them such men as Richard Baxter, John Newton, John and Charles Wesley, John Bunyan, H. C. G. Moule, and others.[8] A study of history reveals that Calvinistic doctrines were unknown during the church's first three centuries. Bishop Davenant, declares:

> It may be truly affirmed that before the dispute between
> Augustine and Pelagius, there was no question concern-
> ing the death of Christ, whether it was to be extended
> to all mankind, or to be confined only to the elect. For
> the Fathers...not a word (that I know of) occurs among
> them of the exclusion of any person by the decree of
> God. They agree that it is actually beneficial to those

only who believe, yet they everywhere confess that Christ died in behalf of all mankind....

Augustine died in AD 429, and up to his time, at least, there is not the slightest evidence that any Christian ever dreamed of a propitiation for the elect alone. Even after him, the doctrine of a limited propitiation was but slowly propagated, and for long but partially received.[9]

Today there is growing division on this issue, most Calvinists insisting that Christ died only for the elect. On the other hand, IFCA International, a group of about 700 independent evangelical churches and 1,200 pastors (some of them Calvinists) declares in its doctrinal statement, "We believe that the Lord Jesus Christ died on the cross for all mankind...to accomplish the redemption of all who trust in him...."[10]

Spurgeon himself, so often quoted by Calvinists to support their view, was torn between his evangelist's heart, which desired the salvation of all, and his Calvinistic beliefs. At times he seemed to reject Limited Atonement, though he often firmly preached it. Sometimes he seemed to contradict himself almost within the same breath:

> I know there are some who think it necessary to their system of theology to limit the merit of the blood of Jesus: if my theological system needed such limitation, I would cast it to the winds. I cannot, I dare not, allow the thought to find lodging in my mind, it seems so near akin to blasphemy. In Christ's finished work I see an ocean of merit; my plummet finds no bottom, my eye discerns no shore. There must be sufficient efficacy in the blood of Christ, if God had so willed it, to have saved not only all in this world, but all in ten thousand worlds.... Having a divine

Person for an offering, it is not consistent to conceive of limited value; bound and measure are terms inapplicable to the divine sacrifice. The intent of the divine purpose fixes the application of the infinite offering, but does not change it into a finite work.[11]

Merit and *value* must apply to the *effect* of the Cross. If the Cross is intended for a limited number (the elect), its merit and value are necessarily limited. "If God had so willed it" is the key clause—which Spurgeon clearly denied at times. On the other hand, that Spurgeon believed salvation was available to all mankind is evident from many of his sermons. The contradiction is clear—a fact that Calvinists are reluctant to admit. Thus I have been wrongly accused of misrepresenting, and even misquoting, C. H. Spurgeon.

1. Duane Edward Spencer, *TULIP: The Five Points of Calvinism in the Light of Scripture* (Grand Rapids, MI: Baker Book House, 1979), 6.

2. R. C. Sproul, *Chosen by God* (Carol Stream, IL: Tyndale House, 1986), 15.

3. Leonard J. Coppes, *Are Five Points Enough? The Ten Points of Calvinism* (Denver, CO: self-published, 1980), xi.

4. D. James Kennedy, *Why I Am a Presbyterian* (Ft. Lauderdale, FL: Coral Ridge Ministries, n. d.), 1.

5. John Piper, *TULIP: The Pursuit of God's Glory in Salvation* (Minneapolis, MN: Bethlehem Baptist Church, 2000), back cover.

6. Spurgeon's Sermons, Vols 1 and 2, "The Peculiar Sleep of the Beloved" (Grand Rapids, MI: Baker Books, 1999), 48.

7. John H. Gerstner, *Wrongly Dividing the Word of Truth: A Critique of Dispensationalism* (Brentwood, TN: Wolgemuth and Hyatt, Publishers, Inc., 1991), 107.

8. Norman F. Douty, *The Death of Christ* (Irving, TX: Williams and Watrous Publishing Company, n. d.), 136–63.

9. James Morrison, *The Extent of the Atonement* (London: Hamilton, Adams and Co., 1882), 114–17.

10. IFCA International, *What We Believe,* I: (3) b (www.ifca.org).

11. "Number One Thousand; Or, 'Bread Enough and to Spare,'" http://www.blueletterbible.org/Comm/charles_spurgeon/sermons/1000.html.

c h a p t e r 3

AGGRESSIVE PROMOTION

CALVINISTS ARE INCREASINGLY INSISTING that their peculiar dogmas represent the faith of "the Reformers who led the Reformation" and should therefore be accepted by all evangelical Christians as true Christianity and as the biblical expression of the gospel. With respect to that...

- ❧ There is much that they stand for with which all Christians would agree.

- ❧ There is much that they stand for with which many evangelicals think they agree because of misunderstandings, but actually do not.

- ❧ There is much that they stand for with regard to the church, Israel, and the return of Christ, to which those who reject the idea that the church has replaced Israel and who believe in the imminent rapture of the church would take strong exception. These latter views have nothing to do with the gospel and therefore will not be dealt with herein.

In the year 2000, the Alliance of Reformation Christians met in London in valid opposition to the influence of the Toronto Blessing in England and sent this message to evangelicals worldwide: "We therefore call upon those who bear the label 'evangelical' to affirm their faith once again in accordance with the witness of Scripture and in continuity with the historic testimony of the church."[1] By "historic testimony of the church," they mean the doctrines that come from Augustine, as interpreted and expanded by John Calvin, and which were at one time forced by a state church upon all in England, Scotland, and those parts of Europe where Calvinists were in control.

An Important Document

Today's Calvinists speak ever more earnestly and boldly about the need for a "new Reformation," by which they very clearly mean a revival of Calvinism as the dominant view in Christendom. Consider some of the resolutions that make up "The London Declaration 2000: Alliance of Reformation Christians—A vision for biblical unity in the modern church, 'The Evangelical Problem'":

UNDER "THE QUESTION OF TRUTH"

We therefore call upon evangelicals to return to the once-held biblical view...that to lay claim to a particular doctrine [Calvinism] as true is not spiritual arrogance but a biblical duty.

UNDER "A VISION FOR REFORMATION"

We therefore call upon evangelicals to affirm a vision for reformation which is in accordance with the witness of Scripture and in continuity with the historic testimony of the [Calvinist] church. Such a vision is of a church which is both *Catholic* and *Reformed*. By "Catholic" we do *not* mean "Roman Catholic".... By *Reformed*, we mean that we confess those doctrines about the authority of Scripture and salvation by grace alone which our Reformed [Calvinist] forefathers reaffirmed at the time of the Reformation [their emphasis].

UNDER "FOUR AFFIRMATIONS"

Under 1: We likewise affirm that we are *Augustinians* in our doctrine of man and in our doctrine of salvation. This is because we believe that Augustine and his successors, including the [Calvinist] Reformers, faithfully reflect the Bible's teaching regarding the total spiritual inability of fallen man to respond to God, God the Father's gracious unconditional election of a people to be saved, the design of the incarnate Son's atoning work as intended surely and certainly to secure the salvation of that people [the elect only], the monergistic grace of the Holy Spirit in regeneration [without understanding or faith on man's part], and the perseverance of the elect. Accordingly, we also reject all forms of synergism or Semi-Pelagianism in which man is accorded a cooperative role in his regeneration [even to believe], e.g. Arminianism. We reject equally any softening of Augustinian soteriology, e.g. Amyraldinianism ("four point" Calvinism), and any hardening of it, e.g. *Hyper-Calvinism....*The notion of one Catholic and Reformed [Calvinist] Church—one main, majestic stream of historic Christian orthodoxy [Augustinianism/Calvinism]—is thus integral to our understanding. This notion we affirm as true and foundational to any evangelical outlook worthy of the name.

Under 2: Reformed Catholics affirm the importance of the church and its history in any authentic vision of God's redemptive work in space and time. Evangelicalism today is infected with a deadly amnesia with regard to the historic [Calvinist] church.... We specifically reject the subjective and often disorderly spectacle of charismatic-style worship, with its attendant practices, such as alleged tongues-speaking, prophecies, "slayings in the Spirit," etc.

Under 4: We bemoan the influence among evangelicals of a pietistic dispensationalism in which the world is considered irredeemably wicked (and thus hardly worth the effort of influencing), and in which the only hope is supposed to be the imminent rapture of the saints.

A Challenge to Remain Silent

With the recent upsurge of Calvinism, a number of leading Calvinists have begun to take a far more aggressive stance in its public promotion. Many on both sides, sadly, are increasingly making this issue a matter of fellowship in the Lord, resulting in division in a number of otherwise sound churches. In some churches, members are forbidden to promote Calvinism even privately. In others, only Calvinists are accepted as members. Of course, the latter has been true of pastors and mission candidates for centuries in nearly all Presbyterian churches and even in some Baptist churches—but now that position seems to be growing and hardening.

Almost daily, I found that this subject was claiming a wider interest and greater importance than I had ever imagined. It seemed obvious that there was great need for further research and writing to deal with this important issue.

As it became known that I intended to write such a book, a number of pastors cautioned me to refrain from publicly expressing myself on this subject. Some claimed that, out of ignorance of its true teachings, I had already misrepresented "Reformed Doctrine." A typical response from the Calvinist friends to whom I sent an early manuscript for comment went like this: "The caricatures you present and the straw men you construct demonstrate to me that you have absolutely no understanding of the Reformed position, and until you do I would counsel that you refrain from putting anything in print." [2]

Letters began to pour into our ministry, The Berean Call, from around the world, many from pastors insisting that I was unqualified to address Calvinism and urging me to seal my lips and drop my pen regarding this topic. It was suggested that I would lose many friends and alienate myself from leading evangelicals, most of whom were said to be convinced Calvinists. Furthermore, who would publish such a book, since the major publishers had brought out many books supporting the other side?

What moved me most was the concern earnestly expressed by close friends that a book from me on this issue could cause division—the last thing I wanted. "We can just hear it now," several friends told me: "Here comes Dave Hunt again; this time he's attacking Calvinists!" That concern weighed heavily upon me.

One must be willing to accept wise counsel. But the advice to remain silent, though given by so many out of genuine concern, seemed, after much prayer and soul-searching on my part, to be ill-advised. Spurgeon called the debate over God's sovereignty and man's free will "a controversy which...I believe to have been really healthy and which has done us all a vast amount of good...."[3] My heart's desire is that this book will be only to God's eternal glory and to the blessing of His people.

1. "The London Declaration 2000: Alliance of Reformation Christians— a vision for biblical unity in the modern church, 'The Evangelical Problem.'"

2. Personal to Dave Hunt, dated October 19, 2000. On file.

3. Charles Haddon Spurgeon, "God's Will and Man's Will," No. 442 (Newington: Metropolitan Tabernacle, sermon delivered Sunday, March 30, 1862).

A CALVINIST'S HONEST DOUBTS

IN THE FOLLOWING PAGES, the questions surrounding Calvinism will be illustrated (compositely as related to me by a number of people) through a fictitious couple, Al and Jan. They've been married almost ten years and have two children. A devout Roman Catholic all of his life, with two brothers who are priests and a sister who is a nun, Al became a Christian a few months after his marriage. After six weeks of struggling to resolve the obvious contradictions between the Catholicism he had known all his life and his growing understanding of what the Bible teaches, Al left that Church, was baptized as a believer, and has been ostracized by his devoutly Catholic family ever since.

Jan, on the other hand, was a typical New Ager who had absolutely rejected absolutes and was open to anything—except, of course, biblical Christianity, which she disliked for being "too narrow." It seemed like a glorious miracle to both of them when Al was able to lead Jan to Christ a few months after his own conversion.

Joy and Fruitfulness

For nearly eight years Al was happy in the faith, witnessing to friends and family and seeing some come to Christ. He was crystal clear on the gospel and the basis of his salvation. There was no doubt in his mind that he had been convicted of sin, of righteousness, and of judgment to come by the Holy Spirit (as all the world is, according to John 16:7–11). Having believed the gospel that Christ died for his sins and that "whosoever believeth in him should not perish, but have everlasting life," Al had placed his faith in the Lord Jesus Christ as his Savior.

At least he was sure at the time that he had believed on the Lord Jesus Christ exactly as Paul exhorted the Philippian jailor, "Believe on the Lord Jesus Christ, and thou shalt be saved" (Acts 16:30–31). As a result (or so it had seemed to him), his life was changed, and this was the testimony he had enthusiastically shared publicly in church and in witnessing to individuals.

From the beginning of his new life in Christ, Al had had a hunger for God's Word as his spiritual food. He had read his Bible regularly with great interest and enjoyment. He and Jan had become part of a seemingly vibrant fellowship of Bible-believing Christians and had rejoiced together in their new life in Christ. Then something happened—a sad tale I've been told by a surprising number of people wherever I have traveled in the world.

Al thought he could not have been happier. He and Jan were more in love than ever with one another and with the Lord. Their children were growing in Christ as the family studied the Word of God and prayed together in their daily devotions, and in the exuberant fellowship of other children at their dynamic church. The only dark shadow was the continued rejection of Al's attempts to witness for his Lord to his Roman Catholic family, and the continued tension that dampened family get-togethers. And then, another disturbing influence invaded their lives, this time from a completely unexpected source.

Enter Calvinism—and Conflict

Almost unnoticed, Calvinism was introduced into a small men's Bible study group that Al attended. Lively discussions followed, which he found intriguing and intellectually challenging. At about the same time, Calvinistic doctrines crept into the pastor's sermons with increasing frequency and fervency. Although the pastor didn't insist (as some Calvinist pastors do) that every church member be a Calvinist, a number of families left the church in protest over the new emphasis. They felt they were no longer receiving the well-rounded biblical exegesis that had attracted them in the first place. Instead, the pastor seemed to bring an unbalanced emphasis upon God's sovereignty into everything he taught—though, of course, he didn't think so. After all, he was only presenting what the Bible said, though with a different understanding than his sermons had reflected in previous years.

It proved to be true once again, as William MacDonald, author of more than 85 books in 100 languages, has stated:

> It is the practice of many Calvinists to press their views relentlessly upon others, even if it leads to church division.... This "theological grid" or system becomes the main emphasis of their conversation, preaching, public prayers and ministry. Other issues seem to pale in comparison. The *system* itself is only a deduction they make from certain verses and is not directly taught in Scripture.[1]

Al was intrigued and swept along with the pastor's new insights. This was the man who had led him to Christ and discipled him, and now Al was eager to follow him into what seemed to be a deeper understanding of biblical truth. Jan, however, was not happy with the implication that God didn't love everyone and had predestined multitudes to eternal suffering, and that Christ had not died for all mankind. She considered such teaching to be directly in conflict both with her conscience and with what the Bible clearly declared. She knew, however, that Al was happy and seemed to be studying his Bible more diligently than ever, so she kept her misgivings to herself.

Burying Contradictions

Seeing his interest, the pastor lent Al some books and tapes by John MacArthur, John Piper, R. C. Sproul, and others. Al began listening to Sproul's daily Calvinist teaching on radio, *Renewing Your Mind*, subscribed to his newsletter, *Ligonier*

Ministries, and bought a copy of the *Geneva Study Bible*, edited by Sproul. Its notes convinced him that Calvinism was the faith of the Reformation and the true gospel. Gradually, the new "truth" began to make more sense, and Al became convinced that what he was learning followed logically from God's sovereignty, a teaching he could now see was neglected and little understood by most of his Christian friends.

That new understanding seemed very comforting. Al became obsessed with God's absolute sovereignty and was greatly influenced by a book by Bruce Milne, in which its author said that God's will "is the final cause of all things...and even the smallest details of life. God reigns in his universe...."[2] Only later would he learn that these words were an echo from John Calvin in his *Institutes*. Of course, the premier writer on sovereignty was A. W. Pink, and it wasn't long before Al was immersed in Pink's *The Sovereignty of God* at the recommendation of Calvinist friends.

It bothered Al at first to think that God had sovereignly ordained everything, even having "decreed from all eternity that Judas should betray the Lord Jesus."[3] Pink explained that "God does not *produce* the sinful dispositions of any of His creatures.... He is neither the Author nor the Approver of sin."[4] Al pondered that idea at length. He was troubled by the teaching that God's sovereignty meant that He controlled and literally *caused* everything, and yet that man was to blame for the sin God caused him to commit. The pastor explained that some things "couldn't be reconciled."

The more Al read, the more the whole matter of man's will became an enigma. He was especially puzzled by seemingly contradictory statements on that subject by a number of Calvinist authors. Pink, for example, rejected the very idea of free will,[5] a concept that he denounced repeatedly. Yet in order to encourage the study of "the deeper things of God [i.e., Calvinism]," he declared, "it is still true that 'Where there's a will, there's a way'...."[6] If God had to make the elect willing to be saved because they had no will, why did their will have any role to play in how much or earnestly they studied the Bible? Such questions bothered Al only briefly and were soon forgotten in the excitement of discovering so much about the Reformation and the creeds it had produced, which he had never known.

Growing Confusion

In order to share his new "faith" with Jan, and to bring her along this inspiring path of learning with him, Al immersed himself in a detailed study of each of the five points of **T.U.L.I.P.** And that turned out to be the start of a downward slide in his faith. Beginning with a deepening understanding of the doctrine of Total Depravity, doubts began to disturb the security Al had once known in Christ. How could he be sure he was truly saved? After all, as a totally depraved person he couldn't possibly have believed in Christ with saving faith unless God had first sovereignly regenerated him. Looking back on his conversion, Al tried to assure himself that that was what had actually happened, even though he didn't remember it that way.

Well, of course, he must have been sovereignly regenerated. That was the only way he could have believed the gospel.

All the Calvinists were very firm on that point. But how could he be sure? After all, regeneration had to happen without his knowledge and before he believed the gospel and was saved. How could he be certain that something he wasn't even aware of when it happened had actually occurred?

If Christ's promise in John 3:16 "that whosoever believeth in him should not perish, but have everlasting life" was a genuine offer to the entire world (as he had once thought but no longer believed), then he could have assurance by simply believing. But if "whosoever" really meant "the elect" and if salvation was restricted to them, his only assurance would be in *knowing* he was among the elect. Was he or wasn't he? That question began to trouble him day and night. He couldn't escape the fear this uncertainty aroused.

First John 5:10–13 ("These things have I written unto you that believe on the name of the Son of God; that ye may know that ye have eternal life...") had once given him great comfort. He had often used the passage to lead others to confident assurance in Christ. Now, however, with his new understanding, Al was convinced that John was writing only to the elect; and if he wasn't really one of the elect, then his believing would be in vain.

Yet all through this epistle, over and over again, it was "believe and have eternal life"—and nothing about being one of the elect. Al took that problem to the pastor, who explained that John was writing *to* the elect, so he didn't need to keep reminding them of who they were. Of course.

Al could not, however, escape a host of questions that began to trouble him. The Bible clearly said that faith came by hearing the Word of God, and one certainly couldn't hear the Word without faith to believe. But the totally depraved couldn't have faith until they were regenerated and given that faith from God. Yet one had to have faith to believe the gospel in order to be saved. So how could one be regenerated before believing and being saved? It was an impossible conundrum.

What "Regeneration" Was This?

There was a brief and heated dispute among his Calvinist friends at the men's Bible study group when Al raised this disturbing question. Various Calvinist authors were consulted, along with the *Geneva Study Bible*, which they all read daily, devouring the notes. There was no question: it was not just a consensus among Calvinist authorities, but unanimous, that regeneration had to precede faith. Before the evening was over, Al was accused of having Arminian tendencies, which he denied, of course, but remained uncertain.

Al became convinced that his doubts had to be an attack from Satan. Could this be what Paul wrote about in Ephesians 6? Al turned there and only became more bewildered when he came to these words: "Above all, taking the shield of faith, wherewith ye shall be able to quench all the fiery darts of the wicked" (Ephesians 6:16). *Taking* the shield of faith? Why would *taking* be necessary if faith were a gift from God, sovereignly bestowed?

There was no unanimity in the discussion group when this question came up a few days later. Al thought that *taking* the shield of faith indicated that faith must involve volition on man's part. Some argued that this was written to believers, and that of course we had responsibility to believe after we were regenerated.

"But isn't it only *after* we've been sovereignly regenerated that God gives us the faith to believe?" asked Al. "Why is that initial faith *without* volition, but afterwards it's different? Wouldn't a faith given sovereignly by God be better than a faith for which we are responsible?"

The lengthy discussion that evening ended without a consensus or further accusations about "an Arminian tendency." Now Al was not the only one haunted by doubts.

1. William MacDonald to Dave Hunt (marginal note in review copy). On file.

2. Bruce Milne, *Know the Truth* (Downer's Grove, IL: InterVarsity, n. d.), 66.

3. Arthur W. Pink, *The Sovereignty of God* (Grand Rapids, MI: Baker Book House, 4th ed., 2nd prtg. 1986), 155.

4. Ibid., 156.

5. Ibid., 1.

6. Pink, foreword to 1st ed. 1918, *Sovereignty*.

chapter 5

A VICTIM OF SUBTLE DECEPTION?

AL WENT BACK OVER SOME of the Calvinist authors he had earlier found so helpful. Now their words only added to his confusion and doubts about his own salvation. Some emphasized Total Depravity to such an extent that the unsaved were incapable of even understanding the gospel. Others, however, like James White, said that the non-elect could understand it but not believe it unto salvation, without the faith God gives. Most agreed that the unregenerate could not believe unto salvation. White made that as clear as anyone:

> It is *not* the Reformed position that spiritual death means "the elimination of all human ability to understand or respond to God." Unregenerate man is...simply incapable [of] submit[ting] himself to that gospel.[1]

Reading those words really bothered Al. If while remaining a spiritually dead lost soul he *could* have understood the gospel, then what he'd thought was faith could have been purely humanistic consent without salvation! How would he know the difference? He had been sure he had understood the gospel and had believed it. But if he had only understood it as a spiritually dead and totally depraved sinner, and not as one who had been regenerated and given faith by God, he would still be lost!

Once happy and fruitful in the Lord, now Al could no longer be certain that his repentance and what he had thought was faith in Christ for salvation had not been purely human emotions. Indeed, that had to be the case unless God had first regenerated him without any act of faith on his part. But that wasn't how he remembered it happening, and he couldn't talk himself into pretending that he had been regenerated prior to what he had always referred to as his conversion.

The Impact of "Unconditional Election"

From his understanding of Calvinism, Al realized that if he had been elected unto salvation, it could only have been unconditionally and thus completely apart from any "faith" he could have placed in Christ. That faith had to be given to him *after* he was saved and could not have involved any volitional belief on his part. But that didn't fit what he remembered.

Looking back on what he had once thought was a clear memory of responding to the gospel by simply believing in Christ, his confusion only grew. He remembered the night he was saved (or had thought he got saved). It was as if a light had gone on when the pastor who had led him to Christ quoted Romans 1:16: "For I am not ashamed of the gospel of

Christ: for it is the power of God unto salvation to every one that believeth." A lifetime of sacraments, confession, penance, prayers to Mary, and wearing of medals and scapulars, suddenly was revealed as useless. The *gospel* was God's means of saving souls, and all he had to do was believe. He had believed the gospel, knew he was saved, and never had a doubt about his salvation for eight happy and seemingly fruitful years.

Al had enthusiastically presented that same gospel to others, believing it was God's power unto salvation if they would but believe. Now he knew that he had been spreading an Arminian lie, which had deceived him into imagining he was saved. And to think that he had deceived others as well! Of course, if they were among the elect, they were saved—and if not, they were doomed, no matter what they believed.

How mistaken he had been to imagine that the gospel was an offer to *him*. What *presumption* on his part at the time! That was the tragic result of hearing the gospel from a non-Calvinist—and now he was *paying the price*. So were those to whom he had passed this misunderstanding in the days when he had been under the delusion that *"whosoever* believeth in him should not perish" meant salvation was an offer to be accepted by anyone who was willing under the conviction of the Holy Spirit.

His pastor tried to encourage Al to believe that his doubts were good—that they helped him obey Peter's admonition to "[G]ive diligence to make your calling and election sure: for if ye do these things, ye shall never fall..." (2 Peter 1:10).

"But how can I make an election 'sure' that I don't have, if I'm not one of the elect?" Al asked in desperation.

"I've seen your works, Al," came the reassuring response. "There are several in our church that you led to Christ."

"Led to Christ? Isn't that an Arminian idea?" Al blurted out in despair. "What do you mean, *led* to Christ! The elect don't need to be led to Christ but are sovereignly regenerated without any understanding or faith on their part—and the non-elect *can't* be led to Christ. How could you have offered me the gift of salvation through the gospel without knowing I was one of the elect?"

"I wasn't a Calvinist then," replied the pastor awkwardly. "Anyway, since we don't know who the elect are, we preach the gospel to all and leave it to the Lord."

"If no one knows who the elect are," demanded Al earnestly, "then how can I know I'm one of the elect? That's what's bothering me! Peter says to make our election sure, but how can I do that when I can't be sure I'm elected?"

"You've got the fruits…," the pastor began, but Al looked at his watch, muttered an excuse and headed for the door, shaking his head in confusion.

"Limited Atonement" Adds to His Despair

The third point of Calvinism, Limited Atonement, further undermined the simple faith Al had once had in Christ. At the moment when he had thought he got saved, he had believed that Christ died "for all…for the ungodly…for sinners…for every man," and thus for *him*. He had thought that Christ's sacrifice on the cross was the propitiation "for the sins of the whole world," and thus it had paid the penalty for his sins.

How easily he had been deceived by an Arminian delusion!

It had finally become the "truth" to Al that Christ's blood was shed only for the elect; otherwise, some of it would have been wasted. Multitudes were already in hell before Christ died. Certainly His blood was not shed for *them*! How could it have been?

Al wondered how he could ever have dared to imagine that Christ had died for *him*! Such presumption must have come from his own pride. Honesty forced Al to admit that he'd never had any proof that he was one of the elect for whom Christ had died. Nor could he imagine how he could ever hope to find such proof.

Al had offered the "good news" of the gospel to friends and relatives and acquaintances. He had told many, with great zeal and confidence, "Christ died for *you*! How can you reject Him when you realize that He loves *you* so much that He came all the way from heaven to pay the full penalty for *your sins* so that He could rescue *you* from hell? If you were the only person on earth, Christ would have died for *you*!"

The Subtle Deception Spread

Now Al trembled to think how many he had deceived. But what could he do about it? He had no way of knowing which ones were not part of the elect. And even if he did, what would be the point of telling them they had a false faith? They were predestined to eternal torment whether they "believed" in Christ or not. They would still end up in hell anyway, and there was nothing he or they could do about it.

Leading others to Christ had once given Al great joy and satisfaction, knowing he would meet them in heaven. Now he knew that the gospel he had preached was a lie that had led many astray, imagining that Christ had died for them. How many he had deceived, he couldn't know, but at least they weren't any *worse* off than before.

Al was now in great despair not only for himself but also for those whom he surely had led astray. Formerly, it had brought him great joy that he had become fruitful for Christ in winning a number of people to his Lord. Now he knew there was no such thing as "winning people to Christ."

It is a delusion of human pride to think that anyone can say "yes" or "no" to God! Whether one will be saved or lost has all been decided by God an eternity ago, and nothing can change that fact. John Piper waxed so enthusiastic about God's sovereignty and the great comfort and joy it brought; and Al had rejoiced over his books. Now God's sovereignty—at least His predestining just the elect to heaven—brought only despair to Al.

"Irresistible Grace"—the Final Blow

The fourth point, Irresistible Grace, had once brought great comfort. Learning that even the faith to believe was all of God had at first seemed so humbling. Now it troubled him deeply. Looking back on his "conversion" as he remembered it, Al could find nothing "irresistible" about his salvation.

Leading up to what he had thought was his "conversion," he had agonizingly weighed the choice between a few more years of sinful enjoyment before eternity in hell, or eternal bliss with Christ. In fact, he had procrastinated after he knew the gospel. Then an auto "accident," which the doctors said he shouldn't have survived, became what he had often referred to in his testimony as his "wake-up call." When the man who was now Al's pastor had presented the gospel to him during his hospital stay, Al had, as he had heard it so often expressed, "given his heart to the Lord." He had believed on Christ and knew he had passed from death to life because of Christ's promise.

That was then—but this was now. Now he knew it all had been a fleshly or even satanic delusion. Yes, he had been absolutely convinced that the gospel was true, and he knew he needed a Savior. He had believed with all his heart that only through Christ's having paid the penalty for his sins could he be saved from God's just judgment. But now he knew that even those who were doomed for eternity could come to such rational conclusions and think they had believed in Christ.

No, he had no proof that Christ had died for *him*—that he was one of the elect. Even less did he have any indication that he had been drawn to Christ by the Father's "irresistible grace." Even now he wanted to believe, wanted to be saved. He felt what seemed to him to be a genuine love and gratitude for Christ's having died in his place. But it had to be the wishful thinking of a totally depraved mind, because he could not identify any time when he could have been sovereignly regenerated prior to what he had thought was his conversion. It simply hadn't happened—he was now devastatingly sure of that!

1. James R. White, *The Potter's Freedom* (Amityville, NY: Calvary Press Publishing, 2000), 100–101.

chapter 6

Something Almost Diabolical

THAT HE HAD READ SOME, though not all, of that imposing and intellectually challenging volume, Calvin's *Institutes of the Christian Religion,* had once given Al considerable pride. One of the things that had first attracted him to Calvinism was the fact that so many of its adherents seemed to be more intelligent than ordinary Christians. They especially gave that impression when they talked about election. He enjoyed the company of the elect, and there was an exhilarating sense of camaraderie in knowing that others didn't understand the truth discovered by Augustine and passed on to Calvin.

Now he turned to the *Institutes* for comfort, hoping that Calvin would offer something to quell his rising fears. Instead, he was horrified. The answers Calvin gave to his questions seemed to credit God with working an almost fiendish deception upon the reprobate, "enlightening some with a present sense of grace, which afterwards proves evanescent."[1] Al was shocked that God would intentionally deceive sincere seekers, and wondered why he hadn't noticed such statements before. (Of course, there were no "sincere seekers"—that idea was just another Satanic delusion promoted by Arminians.)

The deception Calvin attributed to God sounded almost diabolical, leaving Al severely shaken: "There is nothing to prevent his [God's] giving some a slight knowledge of his gospel, and imbuing others thoroughly...the light which glimmers in the reprobate is afterward quenched...."[2]

God Deceives with an Illusion of Choice?

So the totally depraved, dead-in-trespasses-and-sins moral corpses are not completely "dead" but able to have "a slight knowledge" of the gospel, a light God gives them that glimmers and then is quenched, while unable to understand enough to be saved! That *was* diabolical. Yet it rang true to his own experience. How else could he explain that he had once been so sure of his salvation but was now in despair?

Al desperately searched the Bible but could not find any statement about such a difference between the elect and non-elect, especially that in order to deceive them, a false light was given to those whom God had predestined to damnation. Wasn't Satan the one who deceived those who didn't believe, to blind them to the light of the gospel? He read John 1:9 again. It seemed to say that Jesus Christ was "the true Light, which lighteth every man that cometh into the world." He searched Pink's *The Sovereignty of God*, White's *The Potter's Freedom*,

Piper's *The Justification of God*, and the works of other Calvinist authors, but none of them addressed this important verse. Why was it avoided? At last he found where Schreiner dealt with it in detail. Al was excited to read, "This illumination...makes it possible for men and women to choose salvation."[3] Reading on, however, enthusiasm turned to despair. Schreiner was giving John Wesley's "Arminian" view and went on to debunk it. The light of Christ shines upon all men only to reveal "the moral and spiritual state" of each heart, not to reveal Christ to them.[4] Schreiner certainly agreed with Calvin.

It seemed that Calvin was saying that God not only predestined multitudes to eternal doom and there was nothing they could do about it, but He deliberately deceived some of them into imagining that they were truly saved when they weren't! Al could not remember anything in the Bible that would support such doctrine, and noticed that Calvin didn't give any biblical references to back up what he said. With horror, Al read what now seemed to be sadistic reasoning:

> [E]xperience shows that the reprobate are sometimes affected in a way similar to the elect, that even in their own judgment there is no difference between them.... Not that they truly perceive the power of spiritual grace and the sure light of faith; but the Lord the better to convict them, and leave them without excuse, instills into their minds such a sense of his goodness as can be felt without the Spirit of adoption.
>
> Still...the reprobate believe God to be propitious to them, inasmuch as they accept the gift of reconciliation, though confusedly and without due discernment.... Nor do I even deny that God illumines their minds to this

extent, that they recognize his grace; but that conviction he distinguishes from the peculiar testimony which he gives to his elect in this respect, that the reprobate never obtain to the full result or to fruition. When he shows himself propitious to them, it is not as if he had truly rescued them from death, and taken them under his protection. He only gives them a manifestation of his present mercy. In the elect alone he implants the living root of faith, so that they persevere even to the end.[5]

What "God" Is This!

What could Calvin possibly have meant by "present mercy"? No matter how "merciful" God was to these poor souls in this life, could it be called "mercy" at all if its ultimate end was destruction? Was it not cynical to call temporary favor "mercy" upon those predestined for eternal damnation? Who could believe in such a God! Al found himself wrestling with thoughts of atheism and only with great effort suppressed such rebellion.

Luther, too, in *The Bondage of the Will*, seemed to present a "God" who was just as sadistic, "deservedly taunting and mocking"[6] the lost by calling upon them to come to Christ when they couldn't without the help He refused to give them! It is one thing to mock those who, having been given a genuine choice, have willfully rejected salvation and have persisted in their attempt to dethrone God. It is something else for Calvin's and Luther's God, having created man without the possibility of repenting and believing the gospel, to then mock him in the doom to which he has been predestined.

Al could not equate such deceit with the loving, gracious, merciful God of the Bible. But this was the God of Augustine, the premier "saint" of Roman Catholicism, to whom not only Calvin and Luther looked as their mentor but whom so many leading evangelicals praised highly. He was further shaken by this statement in a book he was reading: "The Reformation was essentially a revival of Augustinianism and through it evangelical Christianity again came into its own."[7] To learn that Augustine was the founder of Calvinism and "evangelical Christianity" shook him, as a former Catholic, to the core.

What was the truth after all?

A Desperate Search

Searching for assurance, Al found where Calvin explained that his teaching that some are predestined to salvation and others to destruction was "the only sure ground of confidence [that one was truly saved]," a confidence that only the elect possess.[8] Al thought and prayed about that, but could not see how the belief that God had predestined some to heaven and others to hell could give anyone confidence that he was chosen for heaven. Was he blind, totally reprobate, and unable to see the truth?

His inability to make sense of Calvin seemed to be the final confirmation that he was eternally lost without any hope. The only encouragement he received during those dark days came from the Westminster Confession: "True believers may have the assurance of their salvation divers ways shaken, diminished, and intermitted...by God's withdrawing the light of his countenance, and suffering even such as fear him to walk in darkness and to have no light...."[9] That seemed to bring a glimmer of renewed hope, but he couldn't find the biblical basis for true believers lacking the very assurance that the Bible promises to simple faith.

Then a friend gave him a book that he said had resolved all of his questions. It was *The Reformed Doctrine of Predestination* by Loraine Boettner. The back cover declared it to be "One of the most thorough and convincing statements on predestination to have appeared in any language...the authoritative work in this field."[10] Al began to read it with high hopes. Instead, the book shook him further. The recommendation by *Christianity Today* that "The chapter on Calvinism in history will prove illuminating to many"[11] caused him to read that part first.

Al was immediately troubled by Boettner's admission that early Christian leaders would have rejected Calvinism's view of predestination and that "This cardinal truth of Christianity was first clearly seen by Augustine...."[12] He knew very well that Augustine was responsible for most of Catholicism's doctrines and practices. A recent newspaper article told that the Pope and the Roman Catholic Church had just held some kind of commemorative observance in which this "Saint" had been hailed as the "Doctor of the Church." How could Calvinism be a "cardinal truth of Christianity" if for centuries Christian leaders believed the opposite, until Augustine, the greatest Roman Catholic, "discovered" it?

Is There No Way of Escape?

During the nearly twenty-five years that he had been a Catholic, Al had trusted the Church and its sacraments for his eternal destiny. Of course, under that system of works, rituals, medals, scapulars, and intervention of the "saints," he never could be sure he was saved. The longing for assurance had been a key factor in causing him even to consider listening to what he had been taught from childhood were Protestant heresies.

And now, in his despair, he considered turning back to Rome, even though he knew he'd find even less assurance there than in Calvinism. His former Church had taught him that one never could be sure of getting to heaven; in fact, it was a sin to claim such confidence. He vaguely remembered the anathema pronounced by the Council of Trent upon those who commit the sin of presumption by saying they *know* they are saved and will never be lost.

Now Al understood at last why Cardinal O'Connor declared:

> Church teaching is that I don't know, at any given moment, what my eternal future will be. I can hope, pray, do my very best—but I still don't *know*. Pope John Paul II doesn't *know* absolutely that he will go to heaven, nor does Mother Teresa of Calcutta, unless either has had a special divine revelation.[13]

That was what he needed—a special revelation from God! How else could one be certain, either as a Catholic or as a Calvinist, of being predestined to persevere to the end? Paul had exhorted the Corinthians, "Examine your-selves, whether ye be in the faith; prove your own selves" (2 Corinthians 13:5). Al had thought that was a call to examine his heart to make certain that his faith in Christ was sincere and being lived out in his life through the guidance and empowering of God: "...work out your own salvation with fear and trembling. For it is God which worketh in you both to will and to do of his good pleasure" (Philippians 2:12–13).

But a Calvinist author whom he had read argued from that Scripture, "'It is God who works in you both to will and do.' If this is true after conversion, when I am made free in Christ, it must be even more so before conversion when I am a slave to sin."[14] No further proof was needed of sovereign election. It is God who does all. Then what good would self-examination do? It would never reveal whether one was among the elect. He needed a special revelation from God—but how long must he wait to know it would never come?

1. John Calvin, *Institutes of the Christian Religion*, trans. Henry Beveridge (Grand Rapids, MI: Wm. Eerdmans Publishing Company, 1998 ed.), III: ii, 11.

2. Ibid., 12.

3. Thomas R. Schreiner, "Does Scripture Teach Prevenient Grace in the Wesleyan Sense?" in *Still Sovereign*, 237.

4. Ibid., 240.

5. Calvin, *Institutes*, III: ii, 11–12.

6. Martin Luther, *The Bondage of the Will*, trans. J. I. Packer and O. R. Johnston (Grand Rapids, MI: Fleming H. Revell, 1957, 11th prtg. 1999), 153.

7. Loraine Boettner, *The Reformed Doctrine of Predestination* (Phillipsburg, NJ: Presbyterian and Reformed Publishing Co., 1932), 367.

8. Calvin, *Institutes*, III: xxi, 1.

9. Westminster Confession of Faith (London: n. p., 1643), XVIII: iv.

10. Loraine Boettner, *Reformed*, back cover.

11. Ibid.

12. Boettner, *Reformed*, 365.

13. Sam Howe Verhovek, "Cardinal Defends a Jailed Bishop Who Warned Cuomo on Abortion," *The New York Times*, February 1, 1990, A1, B4.

14. Wm. Oosterman, "Take a Long Look at the Doctrine of Election" (Ottawa, Canada: The Lord's Library Publications, n. d.), 7. Available from Westboro Baptist Church, Ottawa.

chapter 7

"Hyper-Calvinism?" What's That?

AL TOOK HIS CONFUSION back to his pastor again. They had a long talk, which seemed to get nowhere. The pastor could see that Al was near despair. Putting his hand on Al's shoulder, he suggested, "Let's get on our knees and pray about this, Al."

Both of them prayed earnestly that God would clear away all doubts and confusion by His sovereign grace. As they rose from their knees, the pastor went to a bookshelf, pulled out a book, and handed it to Al. It was a well-worn copy of John MacArthur Jr.'s fairly new book, *The Love of God*.

"Don't rush—give it back when you've finished it," he told Al. "I think you've fallen into 'hyper-Calvinism.' This will help."

"Hyper-Calvinism? What do you mean?"

"Well, sometimes it's hard to tell the difference. I guess I'm to blame for leading you into it. I've emphasized Unconditional

Election and Limited Atonement—maybe a little too much—without enough of God's love for the world...."

What Love *Is This?*

"*God's love for the world*? What are you talking about? You can't mean *everybody*...!"

"Well, that's the difference between hyper-Calvinism and the more moderate position that Dr. MacArthur takes in this book. God really does love everybody, and John 3:16 pretty much means what we all used to think it meant...."

"Pretty much...?"

"Well, God does want everybody to be saved...."

"What are you saying?" Al interrupted sharply. "You sound like an Arminian! You know Christ did not die for everybody! Is that what MacArthur says?"

"Of course not! You know he affirms Limited Atonement. Still...he shows conclusively that, contrary to hyper-Calvinism, God has a sincere desire for everyone to be saved...!"

"A sincere desire to save those He has predestined to the Lake of Fire...? That's not what you taught me and it doesn't make sense. Are you pulling my leg?"

"Please. MacArthur proves that God genuinely loves even the reprobate...but with a *different kind* of love than He has for the elect."

"*Different kind of love*? Isn't love of any kind still love?"

"Well, there *are* different *kinds* of love—J. I. Packer says the same, and so does Piper—love for wife, friend, neighbor, even enemy.... MacArthur frankly admits that 'the universal love of

God is hard to reconcile with the doctrine of election...."[1]

"*Universal love*...? Now you *are* pulling my leg!"

"Look, just take this book and read it carefully. It will answer your questions...."

Where's the Difference?

The next evening after supper, instead of going to the men's Bible study that lately didn't seem to be getting anywhere, Al stayed home and began reading the new book with high hopes. The more he read, the more confused he became.

First of all, what MacArthur—and now apparently his pastor—identified as hyper-Calvinism sounded to Al like the very Calvinism he had been taught by the pastor and had learned from books he'd been reading by leading Calvinist authors—and that included Calvin himself. Certainly both moderate and hyper-Calvinists embraced all five points, including limited atonement. Then what was the difference?

Al finally concluded that "hypers" denied that God loves everyone. To them, "For God so loved the world" didn't mean every person "without exception, but without distinction" (a mystifying phrase he now realized he'd been rather proud to interject into discussions with non-Calvinists)—all *kinds* of people that comprised the elect, but not every individual in every kind. But in this book, MacArthur claimed that God loved *everybody*—even the reprobate—and that this was what classic Calvinists had always believed: "The fact that some sinners are not elected to salvation is no proof that God's attitude toward them is utterly devoid of sincere love.... He loves the elect in a special way reserved only for them. But that does not make His love for the rest of humanity any less real."[2]

So God has (or had) a *real* love for those He never intended to save? "What nonsense!" Al muttered, beginning to feel angry. "Why not admit the truth?"

As he read, Al highlighted all the places in the book where it seemed to him that MacArthur contradicted himself, most of which the pastor himself had already highlighted, though apparently in approval. Al showed the pastor the contradictions the next time they got together for their weekly discipleship session.

Excuses, Excuses...

"I think MacArthur is playing a semantic game," complained Al. "He believes the same thing the so-called hyper-Calvinists believe, but he isn't as honest about admitting it! He covers it up with talk about God loving everyone, but that traps him in serious contradictions!"

"How can you say that, Al? He spends an entire book showing from Scripture that God loves all mankind...."

"Yes, and that's the problem! *Loves everyone*? But is it *really* love? Look here: 'He loves the elect in a special way reserved only for them. But that does not make His love for the rest of humanity any less real."[3]

"Yes, that's what I believe. So...?"

"Is it *real love* to predestine someone to eternal torment who *could* have been saved?"

"Well, God isn't under any obligation to love everyone

alike," protested the pastor. "He must be as free as we are to love different people in different ways!"

"It's not a question of *obligation*," persisted Al. "I didn't ask whether God was *obligated* to love everyone. Of course, He isn't—not by any law. He makes the laws. But isn't love His very essence? He *is* love. So His very nature compels Him to love everyone...."

"But not alike in the same way!" interrupted the pastor. "There are different kinds of love. My love for my wife and children is different from my love for my neighbor...."

"I'm not trying to be argumentative. God knows I'd like to get this settled. I'm to love my neighbor as myself. But forgetting that high standard...would it be *any kind of love* for me to set my neighbor's house on fire?"

"Of course not," came the instant and firm reply.

Contradictions...and Double Talk

"Then how can it be love for God to predestine multitudes to the Lake of Fire for eternity? That's double talk!"

"No it isn't. You forget that these are sinners. They deserve it. They hate God, have rebelled against Him...would tear Him from His throne if they could...! God has to vindicate His justice."

"But aren't all men equally guilty and deserving of eternal punishment? If God's justice allowed Him to save the elect, how could it prevent Him from saving all the rest of mankind? His justice has been satisfied in Christ—only for the elect, of course. But couldn't God just as well have chosen to elect everyone, to have Christ die for all mankind, and to sovereignly regenerate and provide all with faith to believe?"

"But that wasn't His plan…" the pastor protested.

"*Plan*? That's the whole point. He *could have* included all in that plan. So how is it love for God to exclude *any* that He could save?"

"That's exactly what MacArthur explains. Let me see that book." The pastor thumbed through it rapidly like someone who had read it several times. "Look here," he said at last: "'Surely His pleading with the lost, His offers of mercy to the reprobate, and the call of the gospel to all who hear are all sincere expressions of the heart of a loving God [who] tenderly calls sinners to turn from their evil ways and live. He offers the water of life to all (Isaiah 55:1; Revelation 22:17)…. Reformed theologians have always affirmed the love of God for all sinners…because the Father loves the human race, and wishes that they should not perish.' Then MacArthur quotes Calvin, who said the same of John 3:16, that Christ 'employed the universal term *whosoever*, both to invite all indiscriminately to partake of life, and to cut off every excuse from unbelievers.'"[4]

Al gave his pastor a long, hard look of disbelief. "That's more double talk…and it convinces *you*? I've read the book. I know what MacArthur says. Turn the page…. Here, let me have it. Look at the end of this quote. Calvin says, 'but the elect alone are they whose eyes God opens….'"

"Of course. If God really wanted everyone to be saved then they all would be. So…?"

Blatant Contradictions

"You don't see the contradiction? God invites *everyone* to salvation—including those for whom Christ didn't die and whom He has already from a past eternity determined not to save and has predestined to eternal torment? Surely MacArthur can't be serious! And you think this makes sense?"

"Just because it seems a contradiction to us...," the pastor began lamely, but Al cut him off.

"You know very well," interrupted Al impatiently, "that you told me many times that Calvinism teaches that God really doesn't want everyone to be saved. He only opens the eyes of the elect! You just said that if He wanted it to be so, everyone *would* be saved.

"Come on, Pastor! That's like issuing a general invitation for everyone in our church to come to my house for dinner but only telling a select group where I live and keeping my address secret from the rest. Of course, my Calvinist friends stick up for me and insist that I really want everyone to come, even though I make it impossible for most people to find me. That's double talk! And it's like that all through this book! I don't know what to believe any more. I want to believe the Bible—but I've lost confidence in it because so many bright men like Sproul, Packer, Piper, and MacArthur claim to find justification in it for the most blatant contradictions."

It wasn't a pleasant scene. The argument became intense, with the pastor defending MacArthur, and Al acrimoniously and impatiently insisting that the contradiction was shamefully obvious and that it formed the very basis of Calvinism. Finally he apologized to the pastor for becoming angry. He regretted having started the argument as he left the church and headed to work.

---

1. John MacArthur, *The Love of God* (Dallas, TX: Word Publishing, 1996), 110.
2. Ibid., 14-16.
3. Ibid., 16.
4. Ibid., 17-18.

chapter 8

ON THE BRINK OF ATHEISM

AL HAD A DIFFICULT TIME all day trying to keep his mind on his job. Cutting through the semantic talk about God loving *everyone*, the truth was that whatever *kind* of love Calvinism credited God with toward the non-elect, it wasn't genuine enough to really desire their salvation. And that meant it wasn't love at all, in spite of MacArthur and Piper writing entire books to try to prove that "offering" salvation to those whom God has specifically excluded from salvation is sincere and loving.

It made Al angry every time he thought of the hypocrisy of "moderate" Calvinists claiming that God sincerely loved those He had predestined to eternal torment when He *could* have included them among the elect just as well as others. Those they criticized as hyper-Calvinists were simply honest enough to admit the truth. Even if God's "common grace" gave the entire world to someone He *could* have saved but instead consigned to eternal flames...there was no way to call that *love*!

Well, this was a general flaw in Calvinism that he had never seen before. Now it was clear. What "God" was this that the Calvinists of all kinds believed in? Al could believe in such a God no longer. Was he becoming an atheist? He knew that couldn't be right—but the temptation to reject God altogether took hold of him and was frightening.

After his conversion, Al had become a strong believer in the necessity of apologetics. Reared in Roman Catholic schools, he had been taught that evolution was true. In university, a debate about evolution between a Christian geneticist and a professor in the same field first started him on an investigation that ultimately played a vital role in his conversion to Christ. He had carefully weighed a great deal of evidence and found that it all pointed to the validity of the Bible and Christianity.

As a Calvinist, however, he had lost his interest in apologetics. Some of his Calvinist friends from the study group were heavily into apologetics—but what was the point? The elect needed no evidence or persuasion, and it would do the non-elect no good. For a time, he felt somewhat confused and even guilty over his change of mind, but that dissipated when a fellow Calvinist (who had been in it longer than he) pointed out from Calvin's *Institutes* where such an attitude was justified.

Calvin's Weakness as an Apologist

It would, of course, be consistent with Calvinism to view evidence and reason as of little if any value in establishing faith. After all, faith is a gift of God given only to the elect after their regeneration. Indeed, why should a Calvinist be concerned (though Al noted that many, inconsistently, were) to offer evidence to the ungodly for the existence of God, and that the Bible is true in every word? The totally depraved cannot be swayed by truth, while the elect don't need such persuasion—since they are sovereignly, without any faith, regenerated in order to cause them to believe—and evidence has nothing to do with that fact. No wonder Calvin had so little use for evidence and proof:

> The prophets and apostles...dwell [not] on reasons; but they appeal to the sacred name of God, in order that the whole world may be compelled to submission.... If, then, we would...save [ourselves] from...uncertainty, from wavering, and even stumbling...our conviction of the truth of Scripture must be derived from a higher source than human conjectures...namely, the secret testimony of the Spirit.... It is preposterous to attempt, by discussion, to rear up a full faith in Scripture....
>
> Profane men...insist to have it proved by reason that Moses and the prophets were divinely inspired. But I answer, that the testimony of the Spirit is superior to reason. For as God alone can properly bear witness to his own words, so these words will not obtain full credit in the hearts of men, until they are sealed by the inward testimony of the Spirit.... Let it therefore be held as fixed, that...scripture, carrying its own evidence along with it, deigns not to submit to proofs and arguments, but owes the full conviction with which we ought to receive it to the testimony of the Spirit.... We ask not for proofs or probabilities....
>
> Such, then, is a conviction which asks not for reasons; such, a knowledge which accords with the highest reason, namely, knowledge in which the mind rests more

firmly and securely than in any reasons...the conviction which revelation from heaven alone can produce...the only true faith is that which the Spirit of God seals on our hearts....

This singular privilege God bestows on his elect only, whom he separates from the rest of mankind...if at any time, then, we are troubled at the small number of those who believe, let us...call to mind that none comprehend the mysteries of God save those to whom it is given.[1]

Objective Proof Essential

It seemed biblical and reasonable to Al that the subjective witness of the Holy Spirit was supported by objective proof. The Bible is filled with evidence. The prophets, Apostles, and Christ himself applied such proof to persuade unbelievers to believe in God and to strengthen the faith of believers. Surely, solid proof ought to be used in presenting the gospel and in reinforcing the assurance of believers.

But what was the point, if the elect alone are given saving faith and that without any evidence but as a result of sovereign regeneration? Then why did Paul and the apostles, following Christ's example, devote themselves to *proving* the gospel (Acts 1:3; 9:22, 29; 10:43; 13:26-41; 17:2-3, 17-31; 18:9-11, 28, etc.)?

Al realized that Muslims could testify to most of what Calvin said about the inner witness of the Spirit. They need no proof, because they have an inner conviction that Allah inspired

Muhammad. Internal and external evidence, however, reveals that the Qur'an is not true and that Muhammad was a false prophet. Mormons, too, are able to hold fast to their "faith" in spite of the total lack of evidence for the Book of Mormon (indeed, much evidence refutes it, such as the video *DNA vs. The Book of Mormon*), because its validity was supposedly verified to them by God through a "burning in the bosom." Such is the secret "faith" of every convinced cult member.

Having belittled proofs, Calvin did go on to offer some, but they were generally weak and hardly sufficient to convince an intelligent skeptic. They involved the majesty of language and sublime truths set forth in Scripture more than evidences for its inspiration. He did touch briefly on a few prophecies, but they were of the kind that were fulfilled in short order, such as the restoration of the children of Israel under Cyrus. The most powerful prophecies fulfilled in Israel throughout history and in the coming of her Messiah were almost completely neglected—the former, no doubt, because of the rejection of Israel as God's people, which Luther and Calvin carried over from their Catholicism.

A Troubling Realization

Calvin did spend several chapters speaking of the evidences that God exists, that the Bible is the Word of God, and that God is the only true God, in contrast to the false gods of the heathen. But why do this if it isn't important? The elect surely don't need any proof. Moreover, the proofs he offered were weak and superficial and would carry little weight with any intelligent skeptic. Many others have written apologetics so far superior to Calvin's that it would seem that he wasted his time.

We do not minimize the witness of the Holy Spirit within the believer. However, the Bible offers proof upon proof, as did the Apostles and prophets. We have the prophecies fulfilled, the historical evidence, and the scientific and logical evidence. These are important in establishing the Word of God and the gospel it contains as the truth of God. Paul told Titus that an elder should "be able by sound doctrine both to exhort and to convince the gainsayers" (Titus 1:9).

Al had not entirely lost his interest in apologetics, but eventually it had seemed of little value in light of his new understanding. Furthermore, he found no hope of apologetics ever being able to prove that he was one of the elect. In fact, there was no way that apologetics could establish the truth of election—much less determine the identity of the elect. That realization troubled him greatly.

---

1. John Calvin, *Institutes of the Christian Religion*, trans. Henry Beveridge (Grand Rapids, MI: Wm. B. Eerdmans Publishing Company, 1998 ed.), III:xxi, 71–73.

c h a p t e r 9

CONFRONTED BY GOD'S LOVE

THE MORE DEEPLY Al studied the subject of assurance, the more confused he became at the frequent contradictions among Calvinists. He read where John MacArthur said that "those whose faith is genuine will prove their salvation is secure by persevering to the end in the way of righteousness."[1] But Joseph Dillow, in a book that had been highly recommended to him by his pastor as giving the clearest word on assurance of salvation, criticized MacArthur and (with many quotations from Calvin to support him) declared that "Saving faith in Calvin and in the New Testament is a passive thing located in the mind."[2] In that case, it would be independent of any works. Then why did it have to be proved by works?

Calvin argued that "If we are in communion with Christ, we have proof sufficiently clear and strong that we are written in the Book of Life."[3] But considering the deceitfulness of every human heart, how could we possibly be sure that we were in communion with Christ—and what about all the other things Calvin said about false assurance from God himself in contradiction to this statement? Al was now exactly where Calvin had said he would be: "All who do not know that they are the peculiar people of God must be wretched from perpetual trepidation."[4] So his wretchedness was, after all, to be endless?

Was He on a Hopeless Search?

Al's confusion only grew (but with it a glimmer of hope) when he read the admission from Gerstner that those who think they have full assurance that they are saved "ground themselves in the faulty definitions of saving faith which we received from the first Reformers. They...defined saving faith as a belief that 'Christ has saved *me*,' making the assurance of hope its necessary essence. Now, the later Reformers...have subjected this view to searching examination, and rejected it (as does the Westminster Assembly) on scriptural grounds."[5] That could only mean that Al's former assurance of salvation had actually been in agreement with the early Reformers, and it was the later ones who retreated from that position! Whom should he believe—and why such disagreement among Calvinists?

Al wondered how he had missed the fact that so many Calvinists seemed to insist that assurance was *impossible*. Kenneth Gentry wrote, "Assurance is subjective.... Dabney rightfully notes that [absolute assurance] requires a revelation beyond the Scripture because the Bible does not specifically speak to the individual in question. Nowhere in the Bible do we learn...that Ken Gentry is among the elect."[6] Al was badly shaken. From Gentry's article and similar statements from other leading Calvinists, was he to conclude that Calvinism actually opposed the assurance he was seeking? That seemed to be what Walter Chantry was saying:

> Few seem to appreciate the doubts of professing Christians who question whether they have been born again. They have no doubt that God will keep His promises but they wonder whether they have properly fulfilled the conditions for being heirs to those promises.... They are asking a legitimate question, "Have we believed and repented? Are we the recipients of God's grace...?" Since we read of self-deceived hypocrites like Judas, it is an imperative question. "What must I do to be saved?" is an altogether different question from, "How do I know I've done that?" You can answer the first confidently. Only the Spirit may answer the last with certainty.[7]

Al was not only confused but also deeply troubled by the very selectiveness of leading Calvinist apologists. In his zeal to deny that volition had anything to do with faith, and to show that it was entirely a mental attitude produced by the Holy Spirit without man's will, Dillow cited Ephesians 6:23 ("Peace be to the brethren, and love with faith, from God the Father and the Lord Jesus Christ")[8] but neglected to mention 6:16 ("Above all, taking the shield of faith..."). Since "taking" surely was something we must do, so believing must be our responsibility as well. But that contradicted the very sovereignty Dillow was declaring. No wonder he hadn't mentioned this verse!

Why So Much Contradiction?

Al found little comfort from his Calvinist friends. They had their own doubts, which they generally denied, only admitting them in rare moments of candor. It was all sovereignty with no part for man to play at all—except that one had to persevere to the end and demonstrate it in one's life. And Al knew he was failing that test.

A friend had given Al an article by R. C. Sproul titled "Assurance of Salvation." Al had read it eagerly, hoping for help, only to come across this troubling statement: "There are people in this world who are not saved, but who are convinced that they are...."[9]

That seemed to describe the very false assurance he once had. Now he knew better. The more he researched, the more convinced he became that assurance of heaven was beyond his reach. And to his surprise, Al was discovering that uncertainty of salvation was rather common among Calvinists. A statement by I. Howard Marshall seemed to go right through his heart, because it was so true of his own situation: "Whoever said, 'the Calvinist knows that he cannot fall from salvation but does not know whether he has got it,' had it summed up nicely."[10] Was Calvinism itself, then, the root of his doubts?

The more Al read, the more confused he became. Dillow went on and on about the faith that brings assurance[11] until it became far too complex theologically for the Philippian jailor to have known what Paul meant when he said, "Believe on the Lord Jesus Christ, and thou shalt be saved" (Acts 16:31). But could it really be as simple as Paul's bare statement?

The Central Issue: God's Love

Al's troubled countenance and increasing moodiness finally provoked Jan to break her silence. "Let me get this straight," she began. "The God you now believe in—"

"What do you mean, 'the God I now believe in'?" Al interjected testily. "He's the same God I always believed in and the One you believe in too!"

"Really? I listen carefully to Pastor Jim...and I'm not the only one with the same concerns. The God of the Bible that I believe in (and you used to) loves the whole world and wants everyone saved. He gives us all the right to choose—so it's not His doing if anyone goes to hell...."

"That's *your* interpretation," interrupted Al. He couldn't let Jan know his doubts.

"Let me finish, please...? Your *new* God gives no one a choice. He regenerates certain elect ones against their will, and—"

"That's not true!" Al shot back quickly. "He makes us willing by changing our hearts."

"Were *you* willing to be regenerated?"

"I didn't know I was being regenerated." Those words slipped out before Al knew it. He had to continue. "That has to come first before anyone can believe the gospel. We're regenerated and then given faith—"

"Exactly what I said. Your will was set against God. Out of the blue He regenerated you. If that isn't against your will...."

"Well...I'll have to think about that."

"You didn't have a choice. He just elected you."

"Grace has to be *irresistible,* because no one wants it. You think a sovereign God is going to let man have the last word! Then He's not sovereign! The God I believe in isn't going to let puny man frustrate His purposes! You don't understand sovereignty...God doesn't share His throne!"

A Selective "Love"?

"Sovereignty, foreknowledge, free will...Calvinists make it all so complicated," countered Jan. "But the Bible is simple enough for a child to understand. The real issue is love—and that clarifies everything. You actually believe that God who *is* love only loves certain ones and predestines the rest to eternal damnation? What love is this?"

"Well...the Bible does teach election. You admit that...."

"Forget election for the moment—"

"It's in the Bible, for heaven's sake! How can you forget it?"

"I mean that's too complicated. There's something simpler—God's love. I can't believe that the God I know sends anyone to hell that He could rescue!"

"It doesn't make *me* comfortable, either. But the Bible teaches this is God's good pleasure."

"*Where* does the Bible say that! My Bible says that God has no pleasure in the destruction of the wicked but wants all to be saved. Al, I love you but I can't go along with this. That's not the God of love I know and read of in the Bible. I think the Calvinism you and Pastor are into misrepresents God. But I don't want to discuss it—we just argue."

"We're not arguing, Jan. This is important. I've been studying this for months."

"Al, I admire you for the effort you've put into it. But it takes no study to see that God loves the whole world so much that He sent His Son to die for everyone's sins, so *that 'the world through him might be saved.'* And that's just one verse."

"*World* there doesn't mean every individual but all *kinds* of people that make up humanity—the elect," Al countered. "You just don't understand. A little more study...."

"Don't you think I've been studying too? I know enough verses to tell me that Calvinism libels the God who Paul said wants 'all men to be saved' (1 Timothy 2: 4) and who Peter said 'is not willing that any should perish' (2 Peter 3:9)."

"*All men* means all classes. Paul says, 'Kings...all that are in authority...' in 1 Timothy 2:2. He's saying there are all classes in the elect. If you'd let me explain—"

"Please, Al, don't complicate the Bible. When it says God loves the whole world and doesn't want any to perish, why work so hard to make it say *elect*?" Jan shrugged her shoulders helplessly. "You go ahead and study Calvinism. I'll stick with my simple faith, and let's not argue about it."

"We're not arguing—just discussing."

But Jan had turned to the kitchen sink and was busying herself cleaning up the dinner dishes, humming, "Blessed assurance, Jesus is mine...."

1. John F. MacArthur, Jr., *The Gospel According to Jesus* (Academie Books, Grand Rapids, MI: Zondervan Publishing House, 1988), 98.

2. Joseph C. Dillow, *The Reign of the Servant Kings: A Study of Eternal Security and the Final Significance of Man* (Haysville, NC: Schoettle Publishing Co., 2nd ed. 1993), 253.

3. John Calvin, *Institutes of the Christian Religion*, trans. Henry Beveridge (Grand Rapids, MI: Wm. B. Eerdmans Publishing Company, 1998 ed.), III: xxiv, 5.

4. Ibid., III: xxi, 1.

5. *Discussions by Robert L. Dabney*, ed. C. R. Vaughn (Richmond, VA: Presbyterian Committee of Publication, 1890), 1:183.

6. Kenneth Gentry, "Assurance and Lordship Salvation: The Dispensational Concern" (*Dispensationalism in Transition*, September 1993); quoted by Robert N. Wilkin, "When Assurance Is Not Assurance," *Journal of the Grace Evangelical Society*, Autumn 1997, 10:19, 27–34.

7. Walter D. Chantry, *Today's Gospel: Authentic or Synthetic?* (Carlisle, PA: The Banner of Truth Trust, 1970), 75–76.

8. Dillow, *Reign*, 280.

9. Cited in Philip F. Congdon, "Soteriological Implications of Five-point Calvinism," *Journal of the Grace Evangelical Society*, Autumn 1995, 8: 15, 55–68.

10. Howard Marshall; cited in D. A. Carson, "Reflections on Christian Assurance," *Westminster Theological Journal*, 54:1, 24.

11. Dillow, *Reign*, 272–91.

chapter 10

HELL: WHOSE CHOICE?

IT WAS DEEPLY TROUBLING to Al (though he wasn't ready to admit it to Jan) that, in spite of the Bible's presentation from Genesis to Revelation of God's love, grace, and mercy to all, Calvinism portrayed God as pleased to damn billions. At one time, this view had seemed the only way to uphold God's sovereignty, but now he wondered whether an overemphasis upon sovereignty had diminished God's love. He read where White said:

> We know, naturally, that we are to have God's glory as our highest goal, our highest priority. So it should not be at all surprising that the most profound answer Scripture gives to the question of "what's it all about" is that it is about God's glory. *All* of salvation results in the praise of the glory of *His* grace.[1]

Those were nice words to which a few months earlier Al would have assented without much thought. Now he wondered how predestining multitudes to eternal torment could be to the glory of God's grace—and how even the salvation of the elect could glorify God if He could have done the same for all, but didn't.

Jan's words from months earlier came back to haunt him: "The Bible teaches that those in hell will be there because, although God didn't want them to go there and lovingly provided and freely offered full salvation, they rejected it."

To say that God's sovereignty would be denied if man had a choice no longer seemed quite as foolproof as it once had. Couldn't God make a sovereign decision to allow all mankind free will? Al began cautiously to read some critics of Calvinism and came across the following, which seemed to make a lot of sense:

> What takes the greater power (omnipotence): to create beings who have no ability to choose—who are mere pawns on God's cosmic chessboard—or to create beings who have the freedom to accept or reject God's salvation? I submit, the latter.... Would a God who ordained the existence of immortal beings without making any provision for them to escape eternal torment be a cruel being? What kind of God would call on mankind to "believe and be saved" when He knows they cannot [and] what kind of relationship is there between God and people who could never choose Him—but are "irresistibly" called...? For these and other reasons I question the idea that individual unconditional election and five-point Calvinism best reflect the attributes of God. A God who sovereignly offers salvation to all through His elect Savior reflects both power and love.[2]

Perseverance of the Saints?

Al continued wrestling with the matter of assurance. Even aside from the question of whether he was one of the elect, he was still confused about whether his experience of trusting Christ was biblical. Reading again James White's *The Potter's Freedom*, he came across the statement once more upon which Calvinists were in almost 100 percent agreement: "[S]omething must happen *before* a person can 'hear' or believe in Christ: and that is the work of God in regenerating the natural man and bringing him to spiritual life."[3] That certainly hadn't been the sequence of events in his coming to Christ, as he remembered it. He had thought that he had been regenerated (born again) *following* his faith in Christ and as a *result* of believing the gospel.

But much like White, Jonathan Edwards also taught that there had to be "the principle of holiness that precedes faith...the alteration made in the heart of the sinner before there can be action [i.e., faith in Christ]."[4] Going back in his memory to that decisive night, Al could not see how that could have been the case.

Al was listening to a tape by John Armstrong, a man he greatly admired as a leading Calvinist, and was shocked to hear him say, "I was asked the question about a year ago by a group of pastors in Pennsylvania...'What do you think is the one doctrine that is the most destructive in the life of the church...today?' And I said, the doctrine of Eternal Security."[5]

Al couldn't believe his ears. He had to rewind the tape and listen to it two more times. Sure enough, he'd heard it right the first time. So the worst thing possible was to have assurance of salvation? Armstrong seemed to explain why any apparent assurance could only be false: "God justifies, but man must have faith and he must obey...(Romans 2:13–14). When it says the one who obeys the law is justified, it means exactly that. That is not a hypothetical verse, ladies and gentlemen, the way many Protestants have read it. And when James 2:13–14 says, 'The doers of the law shall be justified,' it means the doers of the law shall be justified. That's why Paul and James are not in conflict.... Let me suggest...[also] Ephesians 2:8–10.... We are saved unto good works. They're necessary consequential works. Without them there is no salvation. Right?"[6]

No wonder there could be no assurance of salvation: it depended upon our keeping the law! The Bible says no one has kept the law, so who could be saved? Al was devastated. Was Armstrong right or was Dillow? Yet both of them not only contradicted one another but themselves as well. On the same tape, Armstrong said that man had no will, that Luther's *Bondage of the Will* was what the Reformation was all about, and that even the faith to believe was a gift of God. So how could it be man's responsibility to believe and keep the law? Al was bewildered. Nor did it help when Armstrong gave his antidote: "Perseverance, and here's the point, is the necessary attribute of justification."[7]

Forget Assurance

Perseverance? That sure put the burden on him. Did he just need to *persevere?* What good would that do if he wasn't among the elect?

Perseverance was everything for some Calvinists, but not for others. Whom should Al believe? And how could a failure to persevere after the fact prove that one had not been saved in the first place? Why, that would mean that one could *never* be sure he had ever been saved until he died and thus knew whether he had truly persevered to the end! Al had once been so happy with the fifth point of Calvinism because he thought it meant that God would do the persevering: "For it is God which worketh in you both to will and to do of his good pleasure" (Philippians 2:13). Now he discovered that the persevering in good works and keeping the law was up to him, and he knew that he couldn't do it—certainly not if he wasn't one of the elect. That was the question that tortured him.

Why hadn't he noticed earlier this emphasis upon *one's own* perseverance? Al knew that his "performance" had deteriorated lately, and that meant that his perseverance in the faith was far from what it ought to be. That he was plagued by doubts was further proof that he was not persevering. And the doubts only grew the more he studied the writings of leading Calvinists, ancient or modern. Could it be Calvinism itself that fostered the doubts? Perhaps Calvin was admitting this when he wrote:

> For there is scarcely a mind in which the thought does not sometimes rise, Whence your salvation but from the election of God? But what proof have you of your election? When once this thought has taken possession of any individual, it keeps him perpetually miserable, subjects him to dire torment, or throws him into a state of complete stupor.... Therefore, as we dread shipwreck, we must avoid this rock, which is fatal to every one who strikes upon it....[8]

Al was devastated. To try to be sure you're one of the elect would be *fatal*? Wait a minute! Wasn't it Calvinism's doctrine of election that had caused his uncertainty? Non-Calvinists had no such doubts. If he abandoned this doctrine would he find peace?

More and More Unanswered Questions

Al began cautiously to ask Christian friends how they *knew* they were saved. The Calvinists said they were among the elect and had the works to prove it, though at times they weren't especially comfortable with their performance. The non-Calvinists simply replied that they had believed the gospel. Christ had promised eternal life to all who would come to Him in faith, and that was good enough for them.

The more Al studied, the more the troubling questions mounted. If man is totally depraved by nature, how can he aspire to and even do good deeds? But he does. If Total Depravity isn't total in that regard, then why is it total when it comes to believing the gospel? Why would God repeatedly appeal to men to repent if they couldn't? Why send His prophets day after day, year after year, pleading with unregenerate Israel, if they were predestined to rebel and go to hell? If Grace was Irresistible, why not just impart it to everyone? Wouldn't love do that?

Everyone? It always came back to Jan's main complaint—how could God who *is* love allow *anyone* to perish whom He could save? Even worse, how could the God of all grace (1 Peter 5:10) and mercy will anyone's destruction? He had never admitted it to Jan, but that question had long troubled him, and now was beginning to push everything else into the background. Jan's earnest query haunted him: "*What love is this?*"

Somehow, a little booklet by Spurgeon fell into Al's hands, and he was excited to read that even that great preacher and staunch Calvinist admitted that he'd had no perception at the time of his conversion that God had sovereignly regenerated him, nor could he imagine at what point that could have happened. Spurgeon confessed, "When I was coming to Christ, I thought I was doing it all myself—I sought the Lord earnestly...." It was not until some time later that he realized that "God was at the bottom of it all.... He was the Author of my faith, and so the whole doctrine of grace opened up to me...."[9] He closed his sermon declaring that those Christians who are most pious, reverent, and devoted to the Lord "believe that they are saved by Grace, without works, through faith, and that not of themselves, it is the gift of God."[10] That sounded like his non-Calvinist friends and the way he had believed before becoming a Calvinist!

1. James R. White, *The Potter's Freedom* (Amityville, NY: Calvary Press Publishing, 2000), 178.

2. Cited in Philip F. Congdon, "Soteriological Implications of Five-point Calvinism," *Journal of the Grace Evangelical Society*, Autumn 1995, 8: 15, 56–57.

3. White, *Potter's*, 112–13.

4. John Armstrong, "Reflections from Jonathan Edwards on the Current Debate over Justification by Faith Alone" (quoted in speech given at Annapolis 2000: A Passion for Truth conference, sponsored by Jonathan Edwards Institute, PO Box 2410, Princeton NJ 08543). For more information on Jonathan Edwards's view on justification, contact Grace Evangelical Society, (972) 257–1160.

5. Ibid.

6. Ibid.

7. Ibid.

8. John Calvin, *Institutes of the Christian Religion*, trans. Henry Beveridge (Grand Rapids, MI: Wm. B. Eerdmans Publishing Company, 1998 ed.) III: xxiv, 4.

9. Charles Haddon Spurgeon, "A Defense of Calvinism," single-sermon booklet (Edmonton, AB: Still Waters Revival Books, n. d.), 3–4.

10. Ibid., 22.

chapter 11

To God Be the Glory!

AL REMEMBERED THAT BEFORE he'd become a Calvinist he had praised God for being the Author of salvation and the Savior of sinners, had given all credit and glory to Him, and had understood very clearly that he would never have sought Him had God not moved upon him by His Spirit to do so. But he had also been certain that it was his responsibility to respond in faith from his heart. Surely, for man to respond to God by gratefully receiving the gift of salvation would not nullify anything Spurgeon said. And how could it challenge God's sovereignty for man to receive gratefully what God offered while giving God all the glory?

Jan, in fact, had some time previously suggested, "It seems to me that my praise and gratitude to the Lord is more genuine and more glorifying to God than any Calvinist's."

"How can you say that?" Al had protested.

"Because my gratitude and praise comes from my heart. I wasn't programmed to accept Christ—"

"*Programmed*? No Calvinist teaches that!"

"You don't call it that, but you were totally opposed to God, and instead of your heart being won to Christ by His love and grace and mercy, and being *persuaded* by truth under the conviction of the Holy Spirit, you were *made* to believe—"

"Not *made* to believe," Al interrupted impatiently. *When would she ever understand?* "Our wills are changed graciously!"

A Growing Uncertainty

"Okay, you were *caused* to believe. Al, you can't get around the fact that God did something to your will so that you believed what you formerly didn't believe. And it didn't come about by any conviction on your part, any understanding, any faith on your part. I've been reading some of those Calvinist books you've got."

Like every other argument—yes, that's what they had become—this one, too, ended with neither of them giving any ground. But Al was increasingly shaken in his confidence that Calvinism was the truth of God. Most troubling had been the realization that his uncertainty seemed to arise out of Calvinism itself. No wonder Calvin had voiced so many warnings about doubts:

> Among the temptations with which Satan assaults believers, none is greater or more perilous, than when disquieting them with doubts as to their election, he at the same time stimulates them with a depraved desire of

> inquiring after it out of the proper way...I mean when
> puny man endeavors to penetrate to the hidden recesses
> of the divine wisdom...in order that he may understand
> what final determination God has made with regard to
> him.[1]

So it wasn't proper to want to know God's "final determination...with regard to him"? But there was nothing so important! It seemed that Calvin kept contradicting himself. Sometimes he even seemed to say that we should just trust God for our election: "Our confidence ought to go no farther than the word...."[2] Al realized that if he did that he would turn from Calvinism, back to simple faith in the gospel. Perhaps, thought Al in despair, he ought to go back even before what he had thought was his conversion and return to the Church of his upbringing.

Desperation—and Enlightenment

Al began to think more seriously of returning to Catholicism. Embarrassed and uncertain, he went back to his old parish and found that a new priest who didn't know him was in charge. That made it easier. In the process of telling the new man that he wanted to explore possibly returning to Roman Catholicism, somehow the name of Calvin came up. In the next fifteen minutes, to his utter amazement, Al discovered that this priest knew even more about Calvinism than did Pastor Jim.

A well-worn copy of Calvin's *Institutes of the Christian Religion* was pulled from a shelf and the priest began to read a section he was sure would settle any question in Al's mind of returning to the true Church. Al almost jumped up and shouted, "Hallelujah!" when what Calvin had said about baptism was read to him. He could hardly believe his ears that, according to Calvin, his baptism as a baby into the Roman Catholic Church had made him one of the elect. All he had to do was to believe the promise inherent in his Catholic baptism!

Al listened in astonishment and growing assurance as the priest read from Book IV, chapter xv, of Calvin's *Institutes*:

> We have...a spiritual promise given to the fathers in circumcision, similar to that which is given to us in baptism...the forgiveness of sins and the mortification of the flesh...baptism representing to us the very thing which circumcision signified to the Jews.... (IV: xv, 22)[3]
>
> Such in the present day are our Catabaptists, who deny that we are duly baptised, because we were baptised in the Papacy by wicked men and idolaters.... Against these absurdities we shall be sufficiently fortified if we reflect that by baptism we were initiated...into the name of the Father, and the Son, and the Holy Spirit; and, therefore, that baptism is not of man, but of God, by whomsoever it may have been administered [if clergy].
>
> Be it that those who baptised us were most ignorant of God and all piety, or were despisers, still they did not baptise us into...their ignorance or sacrilege, but into the faith of Jesus Christ, because the name they invoked was not their own but God's.... But if baptism was of God, it certainly included in it the promisse of forgiveness of sin, mortification of the flesh, quickening of the Spirit, and communion with Christ. (IV: xv, 16-17)[4]

The Bubble Bursts

So according to Calvin, his infant baptism by a Catholic priest had saved him! Al was ecstatic. The Catholic Church had done more for him than he had known. He was one of the elect after all: Calvin himself had said it! All Al needed to do was to trust his baptism.

But this new assurance lasted for only a few days. Was his faith to be in his baptism as an infant too young to understand anything, and at the hands of a Catholic priest, who himself taught and practiced a false salvation? Was that really the biblical foundation of eternal salvation? Well, Calvin had said so.

What about the true gospel he had believed, "the power of God unto salvation," and as a result had been born again? If being baptized as a baby when he didn't even know what was happening had made him a child of God, as Calvin had insisted, even to the persecution of those who disagreed, then what was the point of his believing the gospel? No, he couldn't accept that after all, even if Calvin had declared it. Al had finally come to a fish in the Calvinism pond too large to swallow.

Now he faced new doubts: If Calvin had been so wrong about infant baptism—and there was no doubt that like Luther he had been—maybe the rest of his teaching was equally false. Why should he believe T.U.L.I.P. at all? It seemed impossible that Calvin could have ever written such heresy as he had about baptism—yes, heresy; there was no other name for it—but the priest had shown it to him right there in the *Institutes*, and Al had looked it up for himself when he got home.

A Forgotten Challenge

Al turned again to his collection of Calvinist writers and began going through their books and listening to their tapes once more, hoping to find the elusive answer he'd been seeking. Tucked inside one of the books, he found a letter received from a concerned friend a few months after he'd become a Calvinist. Now the forgotten and important role it had played in contributing to his doubts flooded his memory. He read it again carefully and thoughtfully:

> As for the doctrine of election humbling you, have you ever considered how you know you are one of the elect? Calvin literally said that God causes some of the non-elect to imagine they have believed and are among the elect, the better to judge them. Is that the God you now believe in? Are you sure you aren't just imagining you are one of the elect?
>
> What qualifies you to be one of the elect? Calvin said there was no reason for God to choose you except that it pleased Him to do so. He also says that it pleased and glorified Him to predestine billions to burn in an eternal hell. Doesn't that bother you? Do you want to accept grace from *that* "God"? I think that's a libel on God's character!

There was more to it—a host of verses (which Al knew very well by now) declaring that God was not willing that any perish, that He wanted all to know the truth and to be set free, that Christ came to seek and to save sinners, not *some* sinners, etc. Al folded the letter thoughtfully and carefully put it back in the book. Originally it had made him so angry that he hadn't answered it. He must reply at last—and much differently from the way he would have responded before. But he didn't want Jan to see the letter or his reply—at least not yet.

The Turning Point

Pondering that letter and how to answer it, Al was struck with the compelling fact that his wife, whom he had "led to the Lord," had the very assurance of salvation that he was seeking. From the very first, when he had been intrigued by Calvinism's intellectual appeal, she had tried to avoid discussing the subject whenever he had brought it up. All she would say was that she was resting in Christ's love and promise and that the gospel couldn't be as complicated as having to change the obvious meaning of words into something else to make God less loving than what the Bible said He was.

What the Bible said! Those words suddenly took on a new meaning and became his deliverance. Getting back to the Bible was the turning point. Al stopped listening to and reading Calvinist and non-Calvinist experts and began to seriously study the Bible itself. It felt as if a burden had rolled off his shoulders just to be able to take the words of Scripture for what they said, rather than having to change them to fit Calvinism.

Among the last issues he wrestled with was Christ's statement, "Ye have not chosen me, but I have chosen you" (John 15:16). In pondering those words, Al realized he was complicating something that was rather simple. Christ was saying nothing more than any employer could say to each employee—that the employer's choosing was decisive. The employee could not force the employer to hire him; but neither could the employer force someone to work for him. Though the employer was completely in charge, the employee had to consent to being hired.

Likewise, we can't force Christ to choose us. He is under no obligation to us; salvation is alone by His grace and mercy and love. But our faith is essential. Salvation is only for those who believe in and receive Christ.

Al took up his remaining doubts with his pastor. They had some long discussions, and in spite of the pastor's efforts to keep him in the fold, Al's faith in Calvinism had been too badly eroded, while his confidence in the simple gospel was slowly being restored. Finally, only one problem remained, which he had to wrestle with on his knees: there was no question that the Bible stated quite clearly that God blinded people's eyes to the gospel. How could that be reconciled with the infinite love that Al now believed God had for all without discrimination?

1. John Calvin, *Institutes of the Christian Religion*, trans. Henry Beveridge (Grand Rapids, MI: Wm. B. Eerdmans Publishing Company, 1998 ed.).

2. Ibid., III: xxiv, 3.

3. Ibid., XV, 22.

4. Ibid., 16-17.

c h a p t e r 12

CALVINISM'S LAST STAND

A FAVORITE SCRIPTURE OF CALVINISTS, and one
to which James White gives considerable attention[1] is John's
comment: "Therefore they could not believe, because that
Esaias said again, He hath blinded their eyes, and hardened
their heart" (John 12:39–40). White also quotes John 8:34–48,
"Why do you not understand what I am saying? It is because
you cannot hear My word...." He then declares:

> Again the Reformed and biblical view of man is pre-
> sented with force: Jesus teaches that the Jews *cannot*
> (there's that word of *inability* again) hear His word and
> do *not* understand what He is saying...they lack the spiri-
> tual ability to appraise spiritual truths.[2]

Far from proving Total Depravity, however, and thus the
necessity of Irresistible Grace, Al could now see that these

passages proved the opposite. If the unregenerate Jews were totally depraved and dead in sins as Calvinism defines it, unable in that condition to see or believe, surely God would not have needed to blind their eyes and harden their hearts. The fact that God finds it necessary to blind and harden anyone would seem to be proof that unregenerate men are able to understand and believe the gospel after all.

But why would a loving God deliberately blind the eyes of the lost, whom He loves, to prevent them from believing the gospel? This seemed especially puzzling to Al in view of God's continual lamentations over Israel for her refusal to obey, and His repeated expressions of desire to forgive and to bless her.

Giving Them What They Want

Since Israel was already in rebellion against God, why would He further harden hearts? There would have to be a good reason for doing this, a reason that would not diminish God's love and mercy; a reason that must apply equally to the Jews in Isaiah's day and yet speak prophetically of those in Christ's day. What could that be?

Inspired of God, Israel's prophets laid out her sin, rebellion, and stubbornness. For example, God through Isaiah laments, "Hear, O heavens, and give ear, O earth:... I have nourished and brought up children, and they have rebelled against me" (Isaiah 1:2). That couldn't be something God had caused—it had to come from their own hearts. God knew their hard hearts and that there was no point in pleading with them further. But He was going to use them to fulfill His purposes declared by His prophets, just as He used Pharaoh.

God would send His Son to reveal His great love, to open the eyes of the blind, heal the sick, raise the dead, feed the hungry, offer Himself to Israel as their Messiah, weep over Jerusalem here on earth as He had done repeatedly from heaven through His prophets in ages past, and die for their sins and for the sins of the world. He would not allow that purpose to be frustrated by a momentary sentimentality on the part of the Jews that might cause them, while still rejecting Him, not to insist upon the cross.

They were going to cry, "Away with Him, crucify Him!" This was what their hard hearts really wanted. And to make certain that they did not relent at the last minute out of humanistic pity, God hardened their hearts and blinded their eyes. So Peter could say, "Him, being delivered by the determinate counsel and foreknowledge of God, ye have taken, and by wicked hands have crucified and slain" (Acts 2:23).

Al could see a similar example in the blindness that will be given to those left behind at the Rapture who have heard and rejected the gospel. Paul states specifically, "And *for this cause* God shall send them strong delusion, that they should believe a lie: that they all might be damned..." (2 Thessalonians 2:10–12). For *what* cause? Because "they received not the love of the truth, that they might be saved...who believed not the truth, but had pleasure in unrighteousness." God would help them to believe the lie their already hardened hearts wanted to believe.

Here we see not a God who arbitrarily blinds people so they can't be saved, but a loving God who is also perfectly just in giving unrepentant rebels the desire of their hearts, which leads to their damnation. They rejected the truth, so God helps them to persist in that rejection. Nor would He need to blind them if they were totally depraved as Calvinism defines it.

Yes, "the natural man receiveth not the things of the Spirit of God...neither can he know them, because they are spiritually discerned [i.e., revealed alone by the Holy Spirit]" (1 Corinthians 2:14). But there Paul is not referring to the gospel that is to be preached "to every creature" (Mark 16:15). He is addressing believers and referring to "the hidden wisdom...the deep things of God," which are only revealed by the Spirit of God to those who are indwelt by and walking in obedience to the Holy Spirit.

The Final Question

Pastor Jim, concerned about Al's weakening confidence in Calvinism, had challenged him: "If you are going to return to the belief that you had the ability to say yes to God in believing the gospel, how can you be sure that some time you may not decide to say no to God—even in eternity in heaven?" Zins expresses that problem as well as anyone:

> It is ironic that many...who adamantly argue that God forces no one to come to Him have no problem believing that God forces those who have come to Him *to stay with Him*. For most evangelicals, free will mysteriously disappears after one chooses salvation...."God will not make you come, but He will make you stay," might be their theological sentiment.[3]

Al asked Jan about this, and her reply was as simple as the Bible itself: "Why would I ever want to give up heaven? There would be nothing to tempt me away from our Lord, who is so wonderful that nothing could!"

"How can you be so sure," persisted Al? "Satan was the most beautiful, powerful, intelligent being ever created. All he knew was the presence of God—yet he rebelled!"

Jan was thoughtful for a moment. Finally she said, "Yeah, but he was never redeemed…never bought with the blood of Christ…. He had no basis for loving God, no gratitude to Christ for dying in his place…."

"So you think gratitude will keep a person from sinning?" cut in Al.

"There won't be any temptation to sin, no reason…it wouldn't make sense."

Al was not trying to argue or put her down. "But who tempted Satan? What was his reason? It was pride. Couldn't those in heaven be tempted to pride if they had a free will?"

Forget Satan

"Al, you keep bringing up Satan. I don't know anything about him…and I don't think we're supposed to speculate about him and his demons. That has nothing to do with us. We are entirely different beings."

She paused again thoughtfully, then continued. "In Romans 7, Paul says, 'the flesh lusts against the Spirit, and the Spirit against the flesh…the two are contrary, so you can't do what you would.' He describes this inner conflict as the reason why Christians sin, if they do, and then he cries out, 'O wretched man that I am, who will deliver me from the body of this death?'—and adds, 'I thank God, through Jesus Christ.' He must be saying that the resurrection, delivering us from these bodies of sin, suffering, and death, is going to solve that problem...."

Al was thinking silently. "That's a good point," he conceded at last. "I guess Satan's example doesn't have much to do with what Christians will experience in heaven. You're right, he was never born again, certainly not indwelt with the Holy Spirit."

After a long, thoughtful silence, he added, "Look, I'm not just trying to argue, as I admit has been the case too often in the past. This is a real problem and I'm looking for honest answers. I want to know the truth...but if we still have free will in heaven, I don't see how...." His words trailed off into a frustrated silence.

Jan gave him a long look of understanding and sympathy. "You really want to know the truth? Jesus said, 'Thy word is truth...I am the truth...the resurrection and the life.' He promised believers eternal life...that we would never perish. I believe Him. That's all I need to know...it's that simple." She smiled lovingly and went back to ironing Al's shirts.

Taking God at His Word

A few days later, it suddenly hit Al like light from heaven that his eternal security as saved by grace depended entirely upon God and not upon himself. Neither salvation nor the assurance thereof is by works, nor can works be a sign of the reality of one's salvation or the means of providing assurance. Even the apparent working of miracles, casting out of demons, and prophesying in Christ's name are no proof that one belongs to Him, as Christ himself solemnly declared:

> Not every one that saith unto me, Lord, Lord, shall enter into the kingdom of heaven; but he that doeth the will of my Father which is in heaven. Many will say to me in that day, Lord, Lord, have we not prophesied in thy name? and in thy name have cast out devils? and in thy name done many wonderful works? And then will I profess unto them, I never knew you: depart from me, ye that work iniquity. (Matthew 7:21–23)

On the other hand, there could be in the life of a particular person not one good work to indicate the reality of salvation, yet that person could be truly saved and thus elected of God to the blessings He has planned for the redeemed of all ages. All of one's works could be consumed in the fire of God's testing of motives and deeds, yet that person not be lost, according to Paul, in spite of no outward evidence of salvation:

> Every man's work shall be...revealed by fire; and the fire shall try every man's work of what sort it is. If any man's work abide...he shall receive a reward. If any man's work shall be burned, he shall suffer loss: but he himself shall be saved; yet so as by fire. (1 Corinthians 3:11–15)

Paul, of course, was speaking of those who are truly saved through faith in Christ. Al could now see his problem clearly:

not one verse in the Bible tells how to know one has been
elected. If being one of the elect is the basis for assurance of
salvation, then there can be no assurance.

But one had to be *certain* about eternity! Yet Calvinists
couldn't agree among themselves on the answer to what was
obviously the most crucial question. Al decided at last that he
was finished with that theory.

Assurance for Eternity

Biblical assurance of eternal life in heaven with Christ rests alone
upon His promises, the promises of the Bible, and upon the foreknowledge, predestination/election, and keeping power of God.
Christ said, "Come unto me," and we came. The gospel says,
"Believe on the Lord Jesus Christ and thou shalt be saved," and we
believed. Christ and His Word promise the following:

* Elect according to the foreknowledge of God the
  Father, through sanctification of the Spirit, unto obedience and sprinkling of the blood of Jesus Christ....
  (1 Peter 1:2)

* According as he hath chosen us in him before the foundation of the world...having predestinated us unto the
  adoption of children by Jesus Christ to himself, according to the good pleasure of his will.... In whom we have
  redemption through his blood, the forgiveness of sins,
  according to the riches of his grace.... (Ephesians 1:4–7)

* For whom he did foreknow, he also did predestinate
  to be conformed to the image of his Son.... Whom
  he did predestinate, them he also called: and whom

he called, them he also justified: and whom he justified, them he also glorified. (Romans 8:29–30)

❧ But as many as received him, to them gave he power
to become the sons of GOD, even to them that believe
on his name: which were born [again], not of blood,
nor of the will of the flesh, nor of the will of man, but
of God. (John 1:12–13)

❧ For God sent not his Son into the world to condemn
the world; but that the world through him might be
saved. He that believeth on him is not condemned: but
he that believeth not is condemned already.... He that
believeth on the Son hath everlasting life.... (John 3:
17–18, 36)

❧ And this is the record, that God hath given to us eternal
life, and this life is in his Son. He that hath the Son
hath life; and he that hath not the Son of God hath not
life. These things have I written unto you that believe
on the name of the Son of God; that ye may know that
ye have eternal life.... (1 John 5:11–13)

❧ Verily, verily, I say unto you, He that heareth my word,
and believeth on him that sent me, hath everlasting life,
and shall not come into condemnation; but is passed
from death unto life. (John 5:24)

We believed, were saved "according to the promise of
life which is in Christ Jesus" (2 Timothy 1:1), and are simply
resting in His abundant promises that "whosoever believeth
in him should not perish, but have everlasting life" (John 3:
16). By simple faith in God's promise (the God who cannot
lie), the believer knows that he has passed from death to life

and will never perish—and he has been given the witness of the Holy Spirit within: "He that believeth on the Son of God hath the witness in himself..." (1 John 5:10). And "the Spirit itself beareth witness with our spirit, that we are the children of God:...heirs of God, and joint-heirs with Christ..." (Romans 8:16–17).

Having "heard the word of truth, the gospel of [our] salvation: in whom also after that [we] believed, [we] were sealed with that holy Spirit of promise, which is the earnest of our inheritance until the redemption of the purchased possession..." (Ephesians 1:13–14). Those who believe on Christ know they are saved and will never perish because God cannot lie. Our trust is in Him for now and eternity.

Paul said, "I know whom I have believed, and am persuaded that he is able to keep that which I have committed unto him against that day" (2 Timothy 1:12). We, too, have believed and know the One in whom we are eternally secure. We, too, are fully persuaded that "the God and Father of our Lord Jesus Christ...according to his abundant mercy hath begotten us again unto a lively hope by the resurrection of Jesus Christ from the dead, to an inheritance incorruptible, and undefiled, and that fadeth not away, reserved in heaven for [us], who are kept by the power of God through faith unto salvation ready to be revealed in the last time" (1 Peter 1:3–5).

We have the many infallible proofs of prophecy fulfilled in Israel (and still being fulfilled before our eyes), and those that promised in detail the coming of the Messiah—prophesies that have without question been fulfilled in the life, death, and resurrection of our Lord and Savior Jesus Christ. We have the historical proofs, the archaeological proofs, the scientific proofs, and the internal proofs that the Bible is God's Word. The Bible offers a true and infallible testimony of the creation of this earth, the fall of Adam and Eve, the redemption through Christ's blood poured out in death upon the cross, of His soon return for His bride, and of His Second Coming to rescue Israel and to establish His millennial kingdom, when He will rule with a rod of iron over the nations from His father David's throne in Jerusalem—and of the coming new heavens and new earth.

We simply believe God's Word in all things, and we are therefore certain that we are saved and that He is coming back to take us to His Father's house of many mansions to fulfill His promise "that where I am, there ye may be also" (John 14:1–3). As Paul said, "...and so shall we ever be with the Lord. Wherefore comfort one another with these words" (1 Thessalonians 4:17–18).

---

1. James R. White, *The Potter's Freedom* (Amityville, NY: Calvary Press Publishing, 2000), 105–109.

2. Ibid., 112–14.

3. Robert M. Zins, "A Believer's Guide to 2nd Peter 3:9" (self-published monograph, n. d.), 3.

A Final Word

MY HEART HAS BEEN BROKEN by Calvinism's misrepresentation of the God of the Bible, whom I love with all my heart, and for the excuse this has given atheists not to believe in Him. My sincere and earnest desire in writing this book has been to defend God's character against the libel that denies His love for all and insists that He does not make salvation available to all because He does not want all to be saved. It is my prayer that readers will recognize that Christian authors and leaders, ancient or modern and no matter how well respected, are all fallible and that God's Word is our only authority.

God's Word declares that the gospel, which is "the power of God unto salvation to *every one that believeth*" (Romans 1:16), is "good tidings of great joy," not just to certain elect, but "to *all* people" (Luke 2:10). Sadly, the insistence that only a select group have been elected to salvation is *not* "good tidings of great joy to all people"! How can such a doctrine be biblical?

It is my prayer that Calvinist readers who may have gotten this far have been fully persuaded to misrepresent no longer the God of love as having predestinated multitudes to eternal doom while withholding from them any opportunity to understand and believe the gospel. How many unbelievers have rejected God because of this deplorable distortion we do not know—but may that excuse be denied every reader from this time forth! And may believers, in confidence that the gospel is indeed glad tidings for *all* people, take God's good news to the whole world!

ALSO BY DAVE HUNT

THE GOD MAKERS
—*Ed Decker & Dave Hunt*

Mormons claim to follow the same God and the same Jesus as Christians. They also state that their gospel comes from the Bible. But are they telling the truth? One of the most powerful books to penetrate the veil of secrecy surrounding the rituals and doctrines of the Mormon Church, this eye-opening exposé has been updated to reveal the current inner workings and beliefs of Mormonism. Harvest House Publishers, 292 pages.

ISBN: 1-56507-717-2 • TBC: B04023

DEATH OF A GURU:
A REMARKABLE TRUE STORY OF ONE MAN'S SEARCH FOR TRUTH
—*Rabi R. Maharaj with Dave Hunt*

Rabi R. Maharaj was descended from a long line of Brahmin priests and gurus and trained as a Yogi. He meditated for many hours each day, but gradually, disillusionment set in. He describes vividly and honestly Hindu life and customs, tracing his difficult search for meaning and his struggle to choose between Hinduism and Christ. At a time when eastern mysticism, religion, and philosophy fascinate many in the West, Maharaj offers fresh and important insights from the perspective of his own experience. Harvest House Publishers, 208 pages.

ISBN: 0-89081-434-1 • TBC: B04341

THE SEDUCTION OF CHRISTIANITY: SPIRITUAL DISCERNMENT IN THE LAST DAYS
—Dave Hunt & T. A. McMahon

The Bible clearly states that a great Apostasy must occur before Christ's Second Coming. Scripture declares that this seduction will not appear as a frontal assault or oppression of our religious beliefs; instead, it will come as the latest "fashionable philosophies" offering to make us happier, healthier, better educated, even more spiritual. As delusions and deceptions continue to grow at an ever-accelerating rate, this book will guide you in the truth of God's Word. Harvest House Publishers, 239 pages.

ISBN: 0-89081-441-4 • TBC: B04414

IN DEFENSE OF THE FAITH:
BIBLICAL ANSWERS TO CHALLENGING QUESTIONS
—Dave Hunt

Why does God allow suffering and evil? What about all the "contradictions" in the Bible? Are some people predestined to go to hell? This book tackles the tough issues that Christians and non-Christians alike wonder about today, including why a merciful God would punish people who have never heard of Christ, how to answer attacks against God's existence and the Bible, and how to tell the difference between God's workings and Satan's. Harvest House, 347 pages.

ISBN: 1-56507-495-5 • TBC: B04955

THE NONNEGOTIABLE GOSPEL
—Dave Hunt

A must for the Berean soul-winner's repertory, this evangelistic booklet reveals the gem of the gospel in every clear-cut facet. Refines and condenses what Dave has written for believers to use as a witnessing tool for anyone desiring a precise Bible definition of the gospel. The Berean Call, 48 pages.

ISBN: 1-928660-01-0 • TBC: B45645

BATTLE FOR THE MIND
–Dave Hunt

Positive thinking is usually better than negative thinking and can sometimes help a great deal, but it has its limitations. To deny those commonsense limitations and to believe that the mind can create its own universe is to step into the occult, where the demons who foster this belief will eventually destroy the soul. Unfortunately, increasing millions in the West are accepting this mystical philosophy, forgetting that it is the very thing that has brought many deplorable conditions wherever it has been practiced. The Berean Call, 48 pages.

ISBN: 1-928660-09-6 • TBC: B45650

DEBATING CALVINISM: FIVE POINTS, TWO VIEWS
—*Dave Hunt & James White*

Is God free to love anyone He wants? Do you have any choice in your own salvation? "This book deserves to be read carefully by anyone interested in the true nature of God." —Tim LaHaye, co-author of the *Left Behind* series. Calvinism has been a topic of intense discussion for centuries. In this lively debate, two passionate thinkers take opposite sides, providing valuable responses to the most frequently asked questions about Calvinism. Only you can decide where you stand on questions that determine how you think about your salvation. Multnomah Publishers, 432 pages.

ISBN: 1-590522-73-7 • TBC: B05000

WHEN WILL JESUS COME?
COMPELLING EVIDENCE FOR THE SOON RETURN OF CHRIST
—*Dave Hunt*

Jesus has promised to return for His bride, the church. But when will that be? In this updated revision of *How Close Are We?* Dave takes us on a journey through the Old and New Testaments as he explains prophecy after prophecy, showing that we are indeed in the last of the last days. In the process, Dave compellingly shows that Scripture illuminates the truth that Jesus will return two times, and that His next appearance—the "rapture" of His church—will occur without any warning. The question is, are you ready? Harvest House Publishers, 251 pages.

ISBN: 0-7369-1248-7 • TBC: B03137

COUNTDOWN TO THE SECOND COMING:
A CHRONOLOGY OF PROPHETIC EARTH EVENTS HAPPENING NOW
—*Dave Hunt*

At last, a book that presents in a concise manner the events leading up to the return of Christ. Dave Hunt, in his characteristic direct style, answers questions such as, Who is the Antichrist? How will he be recognized? How are current events indicators that we really are in the last of the last days? Using Scripture and up-to-date information, Dave draws the exciting conclusion that, indeed, time is short. This book instructs, encourages, warns, and strengthens, urging readers to "walk circumspectly, not as fools, but as wise, redeeming the time, because the days are evil" (Ephesians 5:15-16). The Berean Call, new paperback edition, 96 pages.

ISBN: 1-928660-19-3

A Woman Rides the Beast:
The Roman Catholic Church and the Last Days
—*Dave Hunt*

In Revelation 17, the Apostle John describes in great detail the characteristics of a false church that will be the partner of the Antichrist. Was he describing the Roman Catholic Church? To answer that question, Dave has spent years gathering historical documentation (primarily Catholic sources) providing information not generally available. Harvest House, 549 pages.

ISBN: 1-56507-199-9 • TBC: B01999

Occult Invasion: the subtle seduction of the world and church
—*Dave Hunt*

Occult beliefs march freely across America today, powerfully influencing our children, our society, our government, and even our churches. The deadly impact of Satan's dominion is seen in the rise of teen suicide, the increase in violence, and the immorality that pervades our society. Noted cult expert Dave Hunt reveals: how Satan's lies are being taught behind the academic respectability of science; how demonic activities are presented as the path to enlightenment through "alien" contacts and paranormal experiences; how pagan religions are being promoted through ecology and "we are one" philosophies; and how evil is being reinvented as good by psychology and the legal system. Harvest House Publishers, 647 pages.

ISBN: 1-56507-269-3 • TBC: B02693

What Love is This? calvinism's misrepresentation of god
—*Dave Hunt*

Most of those who regard themselves as Calvinists are largely unaware of what John Calvin and his early followers of the sixteenth and seventeenth centuries actually believed and practiced. Nor do they fully understand what most of today's leading Calvinists believe. Multitudes who believe they understand Calvinism will be shocked to discover its Roman Catholic roots and Calvin's grossly un-Christian behavior as the "Protestant Pope" of Geneva, Switzerland. It is our prayer that this book will enable readers to examine more carefully the vital issues involved and to follow God's Holy Word and not man. The Berean Call, hardcover, 576 pages.

ISBN: 1-928660-12-6 • TBC: B03000

SEEKING & FINDING GOD: IN SEARCH OF THE TRUE FAITH
—*Dave Hunt*

It is astonishing how many millions of otherwise seemingly intelligent people are willing to risk their eternal destiny upon less evidence then they would require for buying a car—yet the belief of so many, particularly in the area of religion, has no rational foundation. With compelling proofs, this book demonstrates that the issue of where one will spend eternity is not a matter of preference. In fact, there is overwhelming evidence that we are eternal beings who will spend eternity somewhere. But where will it be? And how can we know? The Berean Call, 160 pages.

ISBN:1-928660-23-1 • TBC: B04425

JUDGMENT DAY: ISLAM, ISRAEL, AND THE NATIONS
—*Dave Hunt*

In what is possibly the most comprehensive and clear-cut examination of ancient biblical prophecy and modern-day Middle East politics regarding Islam, Israel, and the nations, *Judgment Day!* is an eye-opening page-turner for scholars, analysts, pastors, professors, politicians, and laypeople alike. Amazing historical facts and first-hand insight make this book a thrilling, sometimes troubling, read—but one that is necessary for an accurate understanding of the prophetic times in which we live. Drawing parallels between the "land for peace" appeasement of Hitler (prior to his systematic extermination of more than 6 million Jews) and today's strategy of the nations united against Israel is not at all difficult—but Dave Hunt goes much deeper than that. With painstaking clarity and detail, *Judgment Day!* reveals the ancient agenda against the Jews, and traces its twisted trail to modern-day deceptions of U.S. Presidents, foreign ambassadors, covert (and overt) military operations, businesspeople, educators, and world leaders alike. In this no-holds-barred documentary, Dave Hunt skillfully dissects the myth of Palestinian claims to "the Promised Land," and exposes the fraud, deceit, and treachery of an international community allied against the Jewish nation. As the author writes, "In the final analysis, the battle over Israel is a battle for the souls and destiny of mankind. If Islam and the nations siding with her should accomplish their goal of destroying Israel, then mankind [from a biblical perspective] is eternally lost...." Why are the stakes so high? What will the outcome be? Discover the uncomfortable but irrefutable truth in Dave Hunt's impassioned exposé—*Judgment Day!* The Berean Call, hardcover, 400 pages.

ISBN: 1-928660-32-0

WHAT LOVE IS THIS?

Calvinism's Misrepresentation of God

by Dave Hunt—As the controversy over Calvinism grows, more people than ever are seeking the truth. Explains Dave in the new hardback edition, "The first edition of this book was greeted by fervent opposition and criticism from Calvinists. In this enlarged and revised edition I have endeavored to respond to the critics." Thinking that the only choice is between Calvinism, with its presumed doctrine of eternal security, and Arminianism, with its teaching that salvation can be lost, many sincere, Bible-believing Christians are "Calvinists" only by default. Most Christians are largely unaware of what John Calvin and his early followers actually believed and practiced. Nor do most Calvinists-by-default fully understand what today's leading Calvinists believe. This comprehensive, thoroughly researched and documented resource enables believers to examine more carefully the vital issues involved—and presents a clear case for following God's Holy Word—not man's. (The Berean Call, hardcover, 576 pp.)

[*<u>Honest Doubts</u> is derived from chapters 1, 30, and 31]

TIM LAHAYE

Author of over 50 books and co-author of the Left Behind *Series*

"Every evangelical minister should read this book. If they did, we would see a mighty revival of soul-winning passion that would turn this world upside down as multitudes saw the real God of the Bible, not the false God of Augustinianism and Calvinism."

CHUCK SMITH

Pastor, Calvary Chapel Costa Mesa

"Dave Hunt has . . . stirred the Christian community into taking a serious look at the aberrant teachings...of John Calvin...and thoroughly documents his findings. A must-read for those who...desire to understand the influence that Calvin...continues to have on the Evangelical church."

DR. CHUCK MISSLER

Founder, Koinonia House

"Dave Hunt continues his intrepid commitment to revealing the truth—however unfashionable or politically incorrect it may be deemed. Blind-fold your prejudices and be ready for a stunning and desperately needed perspective on this highly controversial area. Here is another essential for the serious student of God's Word."

DEBATING CALVINISM

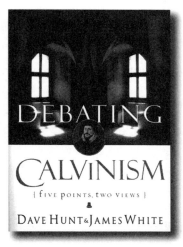

Five Points, Two Views

by Dave Hunt & James White—Is God free to love anyone He wants? Do you have any choice in your own salvation? Two prominent authors examine the validity of Calvinism, which has been a topic of intense discussion for centuries. In this lively debate, two passionate thinkers take opposite sides, providing valuable responses to the most frequently asked questions about Calvinism. White takes the point position; Hunt, the counterpoint. This debate format features affirmative and denial statements concerning the Reformed position on God's sovereignty and man's free will, followed by response, defense, and final remarks. Only you can decide where you stand on questions that determine how you think about your salvation. Engaging reading! (Multnomah Publishers, paperback, 432 pp.)

[additional resources available at www.thebereancall.org]

What Love Is This? (VHS Video)

Does the Bible present a gospel that can only be understood by a select group of theologians? This power-packed video captures the essence of Dave's recent book and provides a succinct historical overview for a careful analysis of the issues involved. Two 45-minute video tapes. (The Berean Call)

Conversations on Calvinism (Audio Tape or CD)

Dave and Pastors Doug VanderMeulin and Steve Watkins engage in a spirited yet gracious discussion on the differing views surrounding Calvinism — challenging and instructive. (The Berean Call, 2 CDs)

About The Berean Call

***The Berean Call (TBC) is a nonprofit,
tax-exempt corporation which exists to:***

ALERT believers in Christ to unbiblical teachings and practices
impacting the church

EXHORT believers to give greater heed to biblical discernment
and truth regarding teachings and practices being
currently promoted in the church

SUPPLY believers with teaching, information, and materials
which will encourage the love of God's truth, and assist in
the development of biblical discernment

MOBILIZE believers in Christ to action in obedience to the
scriptural command to "earnestly contend for the faith"
(Jude 3)

IMPACT the church of Jesus Christ with the necessity for
trusting the Scriptures as the only rule for faith, practice,
and a life pleasing to God

A free monthly newsletter, THE BEREAN CALL, *may be received by sending
a request to: PO Box 7019, Bend, OR 97708; or by calling 1-800-937-6638.*

*To register for free e-mail updates, to access our digital archives, and to
order a variety of additional resource materials online, visit us at:*

www.thebereancall.org

BEND • OREGON